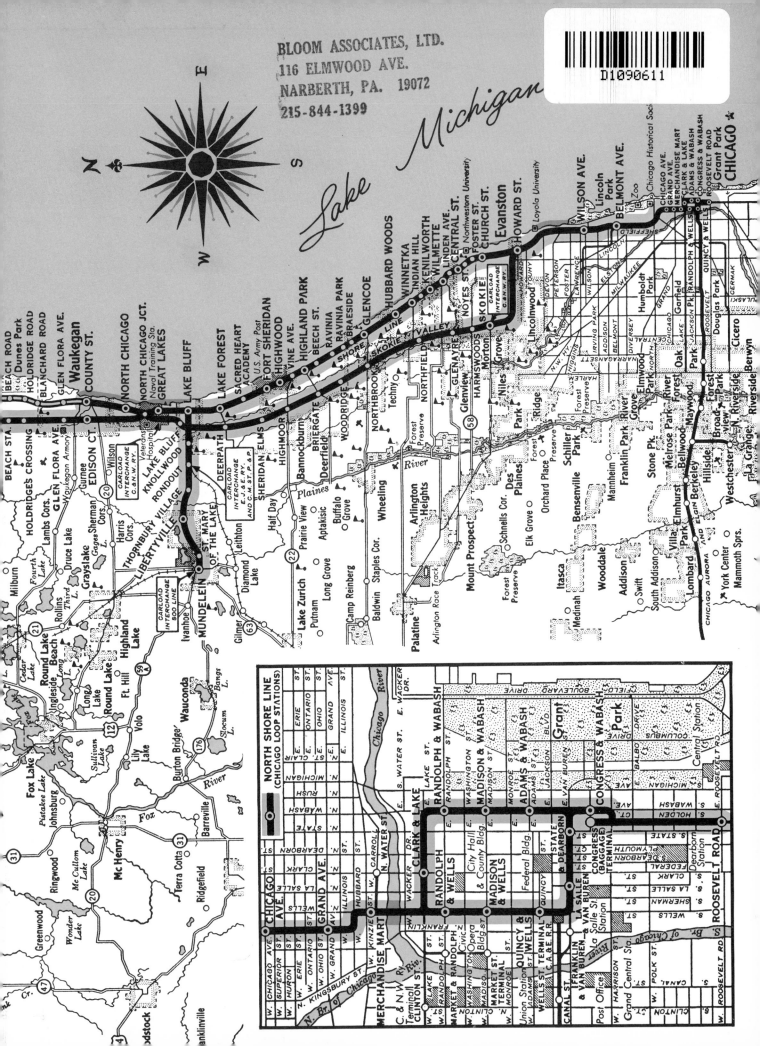

NORTH SHORE

America's
Fastest Interurban

WILLIAM D. MIDDLETON

Golden West Books

San Marino, California

NORTH SHORE

Copyright © by William D. Middleton
All Rights Reserved

Published by Golden West Books
A Division of Pacific Railroad Publications, Inc.
San Marino, California, U.S.A.

Printed in the United States of America
Library of Congress Catalog Card—No. 64-16408

First Printing—April 1964
Second Printing—May 1966
Third Printing—December 1968
Fourth Printing—August 1971
Fifth Printing—October 1973

Credits

Frontispiece—JOHN GRUBER
Title Page—WILLIAM D. MIDDLETON
Time Tables—DONALD DUKE & STEPHEN D. MAGUIRE
Contents Silhouette—A. C. KALMBACH, *courtesy of* TRAINS MAGAZINE

Contents

Foreword

The electric interurban railways must be regarded as one of the more notable business failures of the 20th century, for one can hardly find an industry with a parallel history of such rapid growth, so brief a period of prosperity, or so abrupt a decline. Yet, for a time, however brief, the interurbans filled an important travel need for America; and the fast, frequent, and inexpensive transportation they provided brought a new mobility to rural America and did much to break down the provincialism of the small town. From their earliest beginnings in the 1890's the interurbans had grown by 1917 into a mighty empire of nearly 10,000 cars operating over a network of more than 18,000 miles of intercity electric railways in almost every state of the union. Their decline began soon after World War I, as paved highways advanced across rural America and the family automobile became increasingly common; and before the end of the great depression of the 1930's, the interurbans, with few exceptions, had ceased to play a significant role in American transportation.

Exceptional among interurbans was the Chicago North Shore & Milwaukee Railroad. From extremely modest origins in the early 1890's, the North Shore Line had grown before World War I into an important electric railway linking Chicago with the communities along Lake Michigan and Wisconsin's largest city. In 1916 Chicago utilities tycoon Samuel Insull acquired control of the North Shore and directed its transformation into one of the finest examples of the electric interurban railway in America. In the words of the committee of the American Electric Railway Association which awarded the Charles A. Coffin gold medal to the North Shore Line in 1923: " . . . on this property there has been carried to fruition most of the things that have been talked about for years as the remedies for various troubles." If any interurban could have been called the "standard interurban" in the same sense that the Pennsylvania Railroad once called itself the "standard railroad of the world", it would have to have been the North Shore Line.

The North Shore continued to operate a useful and important transportation service long after the interurban had almost entirely disappeared elsewhere in America; and even when it finally ceased to operate in 1963, its abandonment was dictated largely by economic considerations rather than by a lack of continued public utility.

For me, as for many others, the North Shore Line represented the electric interurban in its finest form. For all who knew it, this volume is presented in affectionate remembrance of the glorious years, now past, when the great steel cars of Sam Insull's interurban raced in majestic and imperious manner over the Green Bay Trail between Chicago and Milwaukee.

To all who have so kindly contributed the wealth of pictorial and historical material of every description, without which preparation of this brief history would have been all but impossible, the author extends the most sincere appreciation. Particular thanks are due to Arthur D. Dubin, O. F. Lee, and Stephen D. Maguire, who have made available rare pictorial material and other memorabilia from their personal collections; to Mrs. Paul M. Rhymer, Curator of Prints at the Chicago Historical Society, who assisted in locating several valuable pictorial items; to Donald M. Steffee, who furnished an analysis of a quarter of a century of North Shore high speed operation; to Lieutenant Commander Lester C. Harlow, who helped clarify early historical details; to publisher Donald Duke, who helped with much of the necessary research, prepared the layout of this volume and added a photographic touch; finally, to camera artist John Gruber, who made available some of the finest contemporary North Shore photography displayed in these pages; to Robert Carlson for his dramatic cover drawing; and to Richard C. Berk for his excellent rolling stock artistry.

Of particular help in the preparation of this volume have been the several publications of Chicago's Central Electric Railfans' Association devoted to the North Shore Line. Notable among these is CERA's 1962 annual, a painstakingly detailed history of the North Shore and its equipment through 1926. The organization's 1963 annual has completed the North Shore story. To all who have a further interest in the subject these volumes are most earnestly commended.

Norfolk, Virginia
May 1963

William D. Middleton

1

Samuel Insull

In the rough-and-tumble business world of the early 20th century one of the most remarkable tycoons of them all was British-born Samuel Insull, who rose from obscurity to forge one of the largest public utility empires of all time. Although his greatest achievements were in the electric power industry, Sam Insull developed one of the finest traction empires of the 1920's, too, and by no means the least of his many accomplishments was the transformation of the Chicago North Shore & Milwaukee Railroad from a more or less typical interurban railway into what was perhaps the finest system of the entire interurban era.

Born in London in 1859 to parents of extremely modest means, Insull began his business career at the age of 14 as a five-shilling-a-week office boy. Largely self-educated, the ambitious youth advanced swiftly in the London business world. In 1881, when he was only 21, Insull was on his way to New York to become the private secretary to a rising young inventor named Thomas A. Edison. Rapidly increasing his usefulness to Edison, Insull was soon managing most of the inventor's business and financial affairs, and in 1886 Edison sent him to Schenectady, New York, to run the new manufacturing plant he was organizing to supply his many electrical enterprises. In 1892, shortly after the Edison manufacturing properties had been merged with the Thomson-Houston Electric Company to create the General Electric Company, Insull decided to set out on his own in the then-infant central station electric power business.

On July 1, 1892, Sam Insull, then only 32 years old, arrived in Chicago to assume a new job as president of the Chicago Edison Company, a small direct current power firm serving only the downtown Chicago area and worth less than a million dollars. During the next four decades Insull built this modest beginning in the power business into one of the greatest utility empires in history.

Under Insull's brilliant management Chicago Edison, which became the Commonwealth Edison Company in 1907 after Insull merged it with the rival Commonwealth Electric Company, quickly grew into one of the giants of the industry and became a leader in the development of the electric power business in America.

Sam Insull applied to the electric business principles which, while they are generally accepted today, were nothing short of radical in their own time. Insull believed in selling at the lowest possible price, not because competition forced him to, but because he believed that lower prices brought greater volume, lowered unit costs of production, and—ultimately—brought greater profits. Thus Sam Insull recognized and applied the principles of mass production, and even coined the term itself, long before Henry Ford got the credit for it. During the 1890's Insull power companies developed the principles for electric power rate-making that became, and still are, the standard employed by the industry throughout the world. In 1902, when the growing demand for power threatened to overtake the capabilities of generators driven by reciprocating steam engines, Insull, despite engineers who said it couldn't be done, persuaded General Electric to construct the world's first large steam-electric turbine. The unit worked, as Insull

knew it would, and the way was opened to even greater growth of the electric power industry.

Well before unions forced enlightened labor relations on most big business, they were a basic Insull principle, not necessarily because Insull was unusually solicitous of his employees' welfare, but simply because he recognized that it was good business to treat his workers humanely and generously, reasoning that a contented work force was less prone to inefficient, costly work stoppages. Insull believed in business growth and expansion, whether by plowing back earnings, by borrowing, or by raising new capital, and Insull companies were among the first to promote widespread public stock ownership. Long before industry in general developed any kind of organized public relations effort, the Insull companies were past masters of the art.

In 1910, once again in the face of opinion that said it couldn't be done, Insull launched a pioneering experiment in Lake County, Illinois, that proved the economic feasibility of rural electrification. Soon afterward Insull, largely through his Middle West Utilities Company, a newly-formed holding company, was embarked on an expansion program that ultimately spread an Insull "superpower" network across much of Illinois and the Midwest.

In 1913 Insull moved into the gas business in a big way when he was persuaded to become chairman of the moribund Peoples Gas Light & Coke Company in Chicago. Applying the usual Insull business magic, he soon had the company back on its feet. During 1929-31 Insull's gas company brought the first natural gas pipeline into Chicago from the Texas Panhandle.

Sam Insull believed that electric transportation would ultimately supplant all other mass transportation media, and beginning in 1914, when the Chicago elevated system came under his control, Insull began acquiring widespread interests in electric railways, and his holdings or systems under his control eventually included Chicago's surface lines as well as the elevated railways, the major interurban railways radiating from the city, almost every interurban of consequence in the state of Indiana, and numerous and widespread lesser properties. Almost every one of these transportation holdings received some measure of modernization and improvement under Insull management, most notably the three major interurbans radiating from Chicago, which were almost totally transformed into superb examples of the interurban electric railway.

By 1930, the Insull-controlled utilities empire was worth somewhere between two and three billion dollars; generated a tenth of the nation's electricity;

and provided electric, gas, and transportation service to some 5,000 communities in 32 states. When the empire collapsed, as it did a few years later, it was perhaps the greatest business failure in world history.

Insull easily survived the onset of the depression, but a series of financial reverses during the next few years brought his long-time financial enemies in for the kill. In 1932, when New York banking interests refused to renew an outstanding loan, Insull's Middle West Utilities was forced into bankruptcy, and the savings of thousands of stockholders were wiped out. Shortly afterward Insull was forced out of the management of his remaining interests. Sam Insull, stripped of his empire, departed for a rest in Europe.

Encouraged by politicians and the press, who could recognize a good campaign issue when they saw it, an intense public feeling against Insull was aroused during the fall of 1932. Insull was charged

with mail fraud and violation of the Bankruptcy Act, and a battle began to extradite him from Greece, where he had taken refuge. Three times Greece refused to extradite Insull, but finally forced him to leave the country. Early in 1934 Insull was seized from his chartered steamship at Istanbul, Turkey, and returned to the U. S. for trial.

During 1934-35 Insull was tried three times, on charges of mail fraud, embezzlement, and Bankruptcy Act violations, and each time he was acquitted. Three years later Sam Insull, the man who had pioneered the American electric power industry and brought cheap power to millions, died of a heart attack in a Paris subway station. Ironically, when the depression was finally over, the Insull companies had proven to be considerably stronger than American business as a whole, and the average stockholder in the Insull empire had lost far less than most investors.

Chicago Tribune editorial cartoonist John T. McCutcheon caricatured Sam Insull's manifold business interests in this 1927 cartoon. COURTESY OF THE CHICAGO TRIBUNE

2

Electric Traction Comes to the North Shore

13

One can, with little difficulty, assemble a rather impressive list of reasons for describing the Chicago North Shore & Milwaukee Railroad as the greatest of all electric interurbans. Surely the North Shore was unexcelled as a high speed, high capacity electric railway. The North Shore's heavy, powerful steel cars raced over a magnificent roadbed on schedules that won it permanent possession of the *Electric Traction* interurban speed trophy, and, indeed, an overseas trade journal once described the road as "the fastest electric service in the world." And it was the North Shore that one June day in 1926 transported the greatest mass passenger movement in interurban history. North Shore limiteds were equipped with sumptuous parlor-observation cars; it was one of the few interurbans to offer full dining car service; and, in 1941, the North Shore introduced the first air-conditioned streamliners on any interurban. Always a pioneer and innovator, the North Shore experimented as early as 1922 with a radio-equipped parlor-lounge car, sold air line tickets at its stations, operated some of the first mechanical refrigerator cars in North America, and, in 1926, pioneered the piggyback movement of truck trailers on flat cars.

But all this comes later in the story.

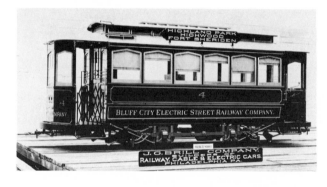

Shortly after its delivery from the J. G. Brill Company of Philadelphia in 1898, the Bluff City Electric's handsomely finished four-wheel street-car No. 3, shown at top of page, posed for photographs on a tree shaded street in Waukegan. Above, No. 4 is depicted in a classic builder's illustration. On the right is shown No. 8, one of the earliest Chicago & Milwaukee Electric interurbans, which was one of two identical cars constructed at company shops in 1901 by splicing together the bodies of two older single truck city cars. TOP OF PAGE AND RIGHT—O. F. LEE COLLECTION, ABOVE— HISTORICAL SOCIETY OF PENNSYLVANIA

14

Considering what the North Shore became, its exceedingly modest beginnings are all the more remarkable. The earliest North Shore predecessor was organized by local businessmen at Waukegan, Illinois, in October, 1891, as the Waukegan & North Shore Rapid Transit Company, and the next year began operation of the first few blocks of what was planned as a seven-mile system of street railways in the city. The original venture was succeeded in 1894 by the Bluff City Electric Street Railway Company, which was soon operating a pair of second hand, single truck cars over several miles of track between Waukegan and North Chicago. Local streets were still unpaved and usually deep in mud during wet weather, and motormen had to be careful to stop their cars exactly opposite the narrow plank walks laid between the sidewalks and car tracks at street corners.

By 1897, when the cars were operating between Waukegan and Lake Bluff, a distance of some six miles, financial difficulties had overtaken the company's promoters. The little line was sold to A. C. Frost and George A. Ball, of Mason jar fame, and reorganized as the Chicago & Milwaukee Electric Railway Company, the new title reflecting the considerably more expansive plans of the new owners. Construction crews pushed southward through the lake shore communities from Lake Bluff, and by 1898 thirteen miles of track were in service between Waukegan and Highland Park. For a time, until the Chicago & North Western relented and permitted the railway to tunnel under its tracks near North Chicago, through passengers were required to disembark from the electric cars and walk across the North Western tracks to board another car for the remainder of their journey. North Western opposition to expansion of the electric line was demonstrated in a more elemental manner at Highwood, where the steam road attempted to prevent construction of a crossing over its Fort Sheridan spur. A steam locomotive was stationed on the spur and its crew instructed to play live steam on the electric line's construction crews whenever they attempted to do any work on the crossing.

In 1899 a ten-mile extension was completed to a point near Evanston, and electric service was extended into a terminal at Church Street in the city over the tracks of the Chicago, Milwaukee & St. Paul Railway. Because of difficulties in obtaining a franchise for operation through the Village of Kenilworth, there was a gap in the Waukegan-Evanston interurban route when operation began, and for a brief period through passengers were forced to take horse-drawn vehicles or walk through Kenilworth to continue their journey on the electric cars.

Passengers for downtown Chicago transferred at Evanston to steam trains of the Milwaukee Road for the remainder of their journey, for which joint tickets were sold by the interurban. An alternate entry into Chicago was developed a few years later

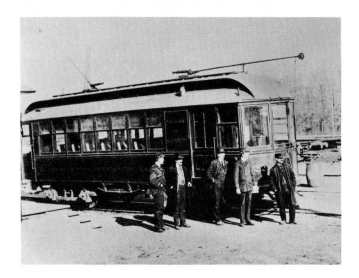

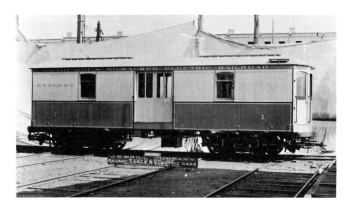

A gallery of Chicago & Milwaukee Electric Railway old timers. At left, a group of trainmen and officials gather around the head end of combine No. 22, one of ten constructed in 1900 by the Pullman works. O. F. LEE COLLECTION Express car No. 1 was manufactured at the Philadelphia plant of J. G. Brill in 1902, when express service was first operated between Waukegan and Evanston. Open car No. 103, one of three delivered by Brill the same year was just the thing for summer trolleying. No doubt because of the poor safety record of conventional open cars which had continuous running boards along the sides, the C&ME ordered cars with a center aisle and vestibule arrangement, and screening along the sides. The gaily striped awnings could be lowered in case of rain. BOTH HISTORICAL SOCIETY OF PENNSYLVANIA Below, combine car No. 14, *Glencoe*, was delivered by Pullman in 1900. After ten years service the car was replaced by larger and more powerful equipment and spent the remainder of its years in work service. ARTHUR D. DUBIN COLLECTION Combine No. 11, delivered under the company's big 1902 order from J. G. Brill, operated in passenger service until 1917, when it was converted to an express trailer for the North Shore's new merchandise despatch service. HISTORICAL SOCIETY OF PENNSYLVANIA On the opposite page, construction forces at Zion, Illinois, push the railway's new Wisconsin Division northward to Milwaukee in 1904. Upon completion of track laying on its new branch between Lake Bluff and Libertyville in 1903, the railway rushed the line into service with open trailer cars and a steam locomotive that had been used in construction of the line. Several months later electric power was connected and a car dragged across the C&NW main line to begin electric service. L. B. HERRIN — COURTESY OF TRAINS MAGAZINE

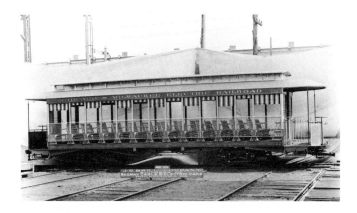

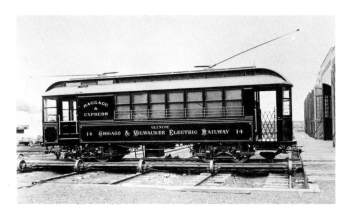

During 1904 construction gangs began extending the Chicago & Milwaukee's new Wisconsin Division northward from Lake Bluff to the Wisconsin state line and Milwaukee. The exceptionally high construction standards employed for this northern extension to Milwaukee laid the foundation for the North Shore's later pre-eminence among high speed electric railways. The double track line was laid with 80 pound rail on white oak ties and gravel or crushed stone ballast. In order to permit unhindered high speed operation a 100 foot right-of-way was acquired and the new route was built through the western limits of the lake shore communities, avoiding operation through city streets. The new line diverged from the original route at Lake Bluff, providing two separate double track routes between Lake Bluff and Waukegan, and between Waukegan and Kenosha sufficient right-of-way was acquired, bridge abutments were designed, and other provisions made for ultimate expansion to four tracks.

While the original line between Evanston and Waukegan had a ruling grade of one percent and a maximum curvature of 14 degrees, the new extension was constructed with a maximum grade of only 0.4 percent and a maximum curvature of only one degree. The entire line was laid on virtually tangent track. There were but two curves in the 20-mile distance between Lake Bluff and Kenosha, and only seven in the entire distance between Lake Bluff and Harrison Street in Milwaukee. Bridges and culverts were of concrete or steel construction and were designed to accommodate locomotives exceeding 100 tons in weight. Crossings with other railroads were made either with grade separations or were provided with interlocking protection.

when the Chicago & Milwaukee worked out a joint ticketing arrangement that routed through passengers via an Evanston streetcar line to Limits carhouse on Chicago's North Side, where another transfer was made to Wells or Clark Street cable cars of the North Chicago Street Railroad Company for the journey downtown.

By 1900, when it owned a total of 43 miles of track and operated 54 passenger cars, the Chicago & Milwaukee Electric had grown into a railway of no little importance. Traffic on the system was already approaching a total of nearly two million passengers annually, and the early years of the new century were to prove ones of tremendous growth and expansion for the electric line.

Construction of the original line had been to the low standards typical of early trolley systems and after still another management change in 1902, when A. C. Frost bought out the Ball interest and reorganized the property as the Chicago & Milwaukee Electric Railroad, a substantial reconstruction of the 25-mile line was undertaken. Curvature was reduced, a second track was installed, and wherever possible the route was relocated to private right-of-way. In 1903 a branch line extending westward from Lake Bluff to Libertyville was opened, and two years later was extended to Rockefeller (later renamed Area and presently known as Mundelein).

Maintenance of these unusually high standards required extensive grading work when construction forces reached the rolling terrain south of Milwaukee. Cuts as deep as 40 feet and as much as 8,000 feet in length were required, and at one point construction crews removed 250,000 cubic yards of earth from a cut 7,000 feet long. Embankments as high as 75 feet were necessary, and one of them required the placement of 500,000 cubic yards of fill.

Said the *Milwaukee Sentinel* of the line on its completion, "It is as near an air line as engineering skill could make it and practically forms one straight run between the two cities. The roadbed is second to none in the United States, not excepting great trunk lines of steam roads."

By late 1905 the new line was completed into Kenosha and the opening of through service between Evanston and Kenosha on December 2, 1905, was

17

On a tranquil summer afternoon early in the century, two big Chicago & Milwaukee interurbans met in the streets of Waukegan on their respective journeys to and from Evanston. By the time these cars were delivered by Jewett in 1906, the line's passenger car architecture had evolved into the handsome pattern typical of the wooden car era on the interurban railways of the Midwest. The view on the left illustrates the superb engineering standards employed in construction of the northern extension to Milwaukee between 1904 and 1908. Except for the installation of heavier rail and ballast during the Insull years, the line was otherwise unchanged in over a half century of operation. WILLIAM D. MIDDLETON

celebrated with appropriate festivities. Three special trains transported county officials, mayors, and aldermen from communities along the line to Kenosha, where the railway company entertained them at a gala banquet served under the direction of the steward who had regular charge of cafe service at the railway's two amusement parks.

With completion of the line into Kenosha, the Chicago & Milwaukee was able to participate for the first time in through service between Chicago and Milwaukee, by means of connections at Kenosha with an interurban line of the Milwaukee Light, Heat & Traction Company and its Evanston connection with the Chicago, Milwaukee & St. Paul. An all-electric route became available soon afterward with the extension of the Northwestern Elevated Railroad into Evanston. Running time for the entire interurban journey between the two cities was about five hours, some three hours greater than the best steam railroad timings, but the $1.25 cost for a one-way journey was less than half the steam road fare.

Expansion of the Chicago & Milwaukee into new territory brought one record year after another. Gross earnings increased steadily to reach almost $600,000 for 1905, over four times the 1900 level. By September 1906 - another ten miles of line had been placed in operation into Racine, and the interurban's earnings for the year increased by almost 50 percent over those for the previous year.

But only a year later the interurban was in financial trouble again. With grading completed into Milwaukee, and track laid to within eight miles of the city, the Panic of 1907 brought a virtual halt to construction work and in January of 1908 forced the company into a bankruptcy that was to last until 1916.

Receivers for the bankrupt railway finally completed construction of the line into Milwaukee and through service between Evanston and Milwaukee was commenced on October 31, 1908, with what the *Milwaukee Sentinel* called an "entirely unostentatious" opening. Indeed, newspaper accounts of the opening were overshadowed by news of the acrimonious charges and countercharges then being aired in court proceedings concerning the involved financial affairs of the bankrupt electric line and its promoter, A. C. Frost.

To celebrate the opening, a special car, carrying the Chicago receivers of the company, was scheduled to depart for Milwaukee from Evanston at 11 a.m. At Racine the Milwaukee receiver of the line was to join the party, and refreshments were to be served during the last leg of the historic journey. Even this modest ceremony was called off and only General Manager R. B. Stearns, who was joined at Racine by an official of the construction company that completed the line, rode the first car into Milwaukee.

Initial service over the 73-mile route between Evanston and Milwaukee was provided by hourly local trains operating on 2 hour 45 minute schedules. Shortly after opening of the line, however, the company inaugurated a four-times-daily extra fare, parlor-buffet limited train service between the two cities which set a standard for high quality service that was to be maintained continuously thereafter for over a half century of electric railway operation between Chicago and Milwaukee.

Nine handsome new interurban cars, designed expressly for the limited train service and constructed to the classic gothic arch window pattern, were delivered by the Jewett Car Company early in 1909. Prior to entering service on February 8, 1909, the new equipment was exhibited to the general public at Evanston and Milwaukee, where large crowds passed through the handsomely appointed trains. Each of the three trains required to maintain the limited schedules was made up of a combination passenger, smoking and baggage car; a coach; and a parlor-buffet car. Constructed of wood, with steel center sills, the cars were 52 feet 6 inches in length and weighed 76,000 pounds. Each car was powered by four 75 horsepower motors.

The combination cars were divided into baggage, smoking, and passenger compartments, seating a total of 42 passengers, with wooden drop seats provided in the baggage compartment for additional seating when necessary. Coaches, which were placed in the center of each of the three-car trains, provided seating for 54 passengers in a single compartment. Interiors of the cars were finished in mahogany, and seats were upholstered in green plush, with the exception of those in the smoking compartment, which were covered in green leather.

Appointments in the parlor-buffet cars were considerably more luxurious than those in the remainder of the new equipment. With the exception of the richly finished mahogany woodwork, interiors of the parlor-buffet cars were finished in a green decor, and the floor was covered with thick green carpeting. Portable wicker armchairs, with green leather cushions and trim, provided accommodation for a total of 27 passengers. Portable tables were available for buffet service, which was provided from a fully equipped kitchen and pantry, and the cars were stocked with Theodore Haviland china, Oneida

A three-car limited train made up of two coaches and a parlor-buffet car is shown above ready to roll out of the Chicago & Milwaukee's Church Street terminal in Evanston on its two hour, 15 minute journey to Milwaukee. The elegant cars were part of a group constructed expressly for the Evanston-Milwaukee limited service by the Jewett Car Company shortly after completion of the line in 1908. Shown below is an interior view of the luxuriously furnished parlor-buffet car. Tables were set with polished silver service, fine linens, and freshly cut flowers. A four-page menu for the buffet service was handsomely printed in color and featured a full page wine list. GEORGE KRAMBLES COLLECTION

Although taken more than two decades later by the successor North Shore Line, these company record photographs provide a good illustration of the well-proportioned wooden cars delivered to the railway by the Jewett Car Company under a series of orders between 1906 and 1909. Coach accommodations on the Chicago & Milwaukee were evidently somewhat on the utilitarian side.
BOTH O. F. LEE COLLECTION

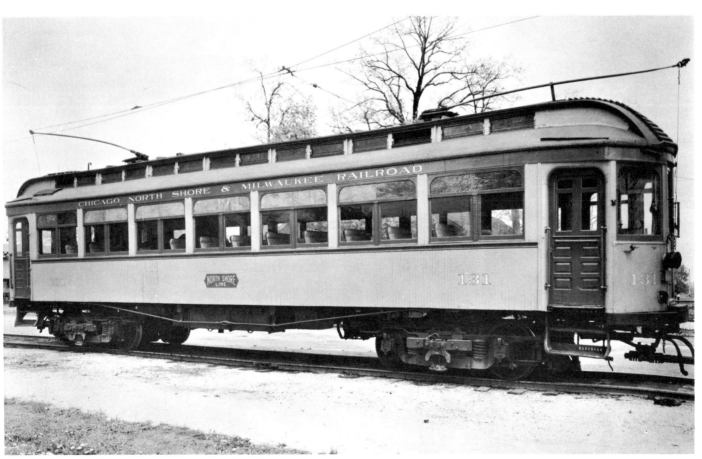

The company's magnificent Ravinia Park was a popular year-around attraction. Illustrated above are views of the Music Pavilon, Theater, Stadium, and Casino as they appeared in a 1906 issue of the *Street Railway Journal.* DONALD DUKE COLLECTION Equipment of the connecting Northwestern Elevated Railroad was frequently employed to accommodate special movements to Ravinia Park during the summer months. Below, one of the railway's steeple cab locomotives arrives at the park with a 12-car train of "L" equipment. ARTHUR D. DUBIN COLLECTION

silver, and the finest cut glass and linens. Each of the cars was staffed with a cook and two waiters, and an extensive buffet menu and wine list, described as equivalent to those of a first class Pullman service, were offered. The facilities of the parlor-buffet car were available to all passengers on the limited trains, who paid an extra fare which varied from five cents to 25 cents, depending upon the distance traveled.

Schedules for the limited train service, which was operated at three-hour intervals from 8:30 a.m. to 5:30 p.m., allowed 2 hours 15 minutes for the 73-mile journey between Evanston and Milwaukee. The limited service supplemented an additional 14 local trains operated in each direction between the two cities on 2 hour 45 minute schedules. The railway's new luxury service proved to be extremely popular with the public, and by July 1910, the extra-fare limiteds were carrying about 31,000 passengers a month, an average of 125 passengers on each trip.

Early interurban railway operators often found excursion business to be a lucrative source of extra income, and the Chicago & Milwaukee was easily among the most resourceful and successful promoters of such traffic. Railway-owned amusement parks, located far enough from town to require a trip on the cars, were a common device to promote pleasure travel, and the Chicago & Milwaukee constructed two of them early in its history.

The company's Fort Sheridan Park at Highwood was more or less typical of electric railway amusement parks, including among its attractions such features as an open air park, a dance hall, a beer garden, and a theatre. The big celebration that opened the park in 1901 featured an 18-piece Mexican band which played throughout the day and far into the night.

The company's magnificent Ravinia Park, near Glencoe, was quite another matter. Located on 42

acres of woodland 11 miles north of Evanston, the park was planned for year-around operation, and its features were intended to appeal only to the highest class of patrons. Among the park's handsome structures was a theatre seating over 1,000, where such performances as the Burton-Holmes lecture series, concerts by the Theodore Thomas Orchestra, and similar high quality entertainments were given. Special cars were run from Evanston and Waukegan for evening performances at the theatre. A large casino building included a cafe, ladies' retiring rooms, men's smoking rooms, and a ball room, which was available for rental to private parties. Such distinguished attractions as the Damrosch New York Symphony Orchestra, which appeared at Ravinia during 1905 and 1906, drew as many as 7,500 people for performances in the park's music pavillion.

A stadium with a seating capacity of 2,000 was provided for baseball, football, and other contests. Winter crowds were attracted by means of a three-acre skating park and a toboggan slide; and winter season family tickets, which admitted up to ten people, were sold for only $5.00.

The high class character of Ravinia Park was carefully maintained by the railway, which scrupulously refrained from providing anything at all that might attract the "undesirable element." No intoxicating liquors whatever were sold on the grounds, and "attractions of the cheaper variety, such as palm reading, cheap shows, and gaming devices" were entirely absent. In later years the park, which still operates, became the summer home of the Chicago Symphony Orchestra, and regular opera performances were held during the summer. On such occasions the railway operated special trains direct from Chicago to the park. Special tickets for the excursions included both the rail fare and admission to the park, and a light supper was served during the return trip.

Above, a bird's-eye view of Ravina Park. DONALD
DUKE COLLECTON The views below illustrate how
the big wooden Jewett interurbans were used to
haul open trailers on special outings to Ravina
Park early in the century.

The company also made vigorous efforts to develop other excursion business, and to encourage special party movements. The railway's traffic department built up an extensive mailing list from such sources as Sunday school publishing houses, clubs, and other directories, and each year sent out hundreds of circulars calling attention to special points of interest along the line, and the services available from the railway. Special excursions were widely publicized in local newspaper advertisements, which included special coupons good for reduced rate tickets. In 1911 over 30,000 extra passengers were solicited by this method alone.

Despite the extended bankruptcy that began in 1908, the Chicago & Milwaukee made modest gains in traffic following completion of the route to Milwaukee. Sixteen new interurban cars were delivered in 1910 to help accommodate the growing traffic, and by 1911 the company was earning an annual net income of almost a quarter of a million dollars. A serious handicap to a greater development of the company's traffic, however, was the lack of a direct entrance into downtown Chicago. In addition to the inconvenience of changing trains at Evanston, interurban passengers were faced with an elevated train journey of over an hour to reach the Loop. As long as this condition prevailed, suburban traffic between Chicago and the North Shore communities remained almost entirely in the hands of the steam railroads.

As early as 1906, when the Northwestern Elevated Railroad was being extended from Wilson Avenue into Evanston over a branch of the Chicago, Milwaukee & St. Paul Railway, it was considered probable that interurban trains would soon be operating into the Loop over "L" tracks, and the company even leased property at Second and Wells Streets in Chicago on which to locate its downtown terminal. Work on this project was deferred, however, until after completion of the interurban's line into Milwaukee, by which time the company was bankrupt.

Other proposals for a Chicago entrance were advanced in subsequent years. At one time it was proposed that an extension be built to connect the interurban with the Logan Square branch of the Metropolitan West Side Elevated Railroad. In 1911 rumor even had it that the bankrupt interurban would be merged with the Northwestern Elevated Railroad and the trains would at last begin operating into the Loop.

It became increasingly evident, however, that negotiation of a suitable agreement for operation of Chicago & Milwaukee trains into downtown Chicago would have to wait until after reorganization of the company and the restoration of more stable operating conditions, and this became the principal consideration in efforts to bring the receivership to a speedy termination. The company's tangled financial affairs proved difficult to settle, and the resulting litigation kept the Chicago & Milwaukee in bankruptcy court for over eight years. Before the

long receivership was over, some 85 lawyers or law firms had appeared in the court proceedings; and it was estimated that nearly a million dollars had been spent in legal fees.

Among those interested in the bankrupt interurban was Chicago utilities tycoon Samuel Insull, who made a detailed inspection trip over the line as early as September 1911. Insull, whose interests in traction properties had previously been confined largely to those which were more or less incidental adjuncts to his extensive utility holdings, had begun to take a greater interest in electric railways about this time. His Commonwealth Edison Company earlier in 1911 had become the financial power behind a move to merge Chicago's elevated railways, and within three years the Insull power company was the owner of the consolidated system. Soon afterward Insull began to acquire control of the interurban railways radiating from the city, and to modernize and coordinate them.

An initial Insull move to acquire the Chicago & Milwaukee in 1912 failed, when the courts nullified sale of the property to Insull because the price was too low. Eventually, agreement was reached on a reorganization plan for the bankrupt railway; and on May 1, 1916, the Chicago & Milwaukee was sold to an Insull-backed reorganization committee for a total of $4,550,000 and promptly reorganized as the Chicago North Shore & Milwaukee Railroad.

Sam Insull was in charge now and the stage was set for a remarkable decade of reconstruction and expansion that would transform the new North Shore Line into the dazzling wonder of the traction world.

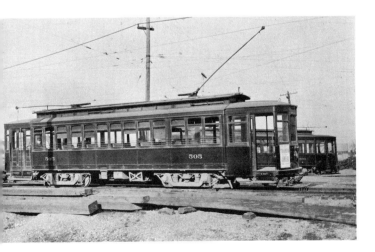

Ten roomy, *pay-as-you-enter* city cars for the railway's Milwaukee local line were delivered by the St. Louis Car Company in 1909. Interiors of the 52-seat cars were finished in mahogany stained birch and birdseye maple headlining, and the deck sash was fitted with Florentine glass. Above, No. 501 and an interurban car lay over outside the Harrison Street car barn at Milwaukee. Below, No. 505 waits at the car barn for a northbound trip.
BOTH PAUL STRINGHAM COLLECTION

3
The Insull Years

The Insull modernization program for the North Shore, which began almost immediately upon establishment of the new company on July 26, 1916, came at a fortuitous time for the railway. Less than a year later America was to enter World War I; and a general quickening of business activity, together with a tremendous expansion of two major military training centers along the North Shore, the Army's Fort Sheridan at Highwood and the Navy's Great Lakes Training Station at North Chicago, brought a substantial increase in traffic for which the new company was well prepared.

Sam Insull himself became chairman of the board of the new North Shore, while one of his ablest lieutenants, Britton I. Budd, was elected president of the company and actually directed the Insull reconstruction program. Budd, then 42 years old, had begun 17 years earlier as an assistant storekeeper on the Metropolitan Elevated Railway Company. By the time Insull assumed control of the Chicago elevated railways in 1914, Budd was president of the Metropolitan, and Insull picked him to head the new consolidated elevated system. "I got all the heads of the elevated lines together and looked them over," Insull later recalled. "Budd was by far the most likely looking of them." Under Budd's skillful management, elevated operations were coordinated, and substantial improvements were made to the system. One enthusiastic newspaper writer went so far as to describe Budd as a "Moses for the

Britton I. Budd, one of Insull's most capable managers, became president of the North Shore following the 1916 reorganization, and directed the railway's transformation into one of America's finest interurban systems. CHICAGO HISTORICAL SOCIETY Although actually delivered to the railway a year before the Insull management assumed control, a group of 15 steel interurban cars built by J. G. Brill in 1915 established the basic pattern for a North Shore steel car fleet that was to reach a total of 145 units by 1930. DONALD DUKE COLLECTION

Four 140 horsepower motors powered each of the big, 45-ton steel cars which were capable of speeds in the vicinity of 80 m.p.h. Although many refinements and improvements were made in the design, the same general dimensions, motors and controls were employed in subsequent car orders over the next 15 years. MAX E. WILCOX COLLECTION Seats in the smoking compartment, shown in the interior view above, were covered in rattan, while those in the main compartment were upholstered in red plush. Visible are such typical appurtenances as the conductor's fare register and a case containing rescue tools. HISTORICAL SOCIETY OF PENNSYLVANIA

tractions," and a letter writer to the *Chicago Tribune* proclaimed, "Praise Budd from Whom All Blessings Flow."

In subsequent years, as Insull acquired control of the other interurbans radiating from Chicago, the capable Budd managed them as well. And when Insull needed a new operating head for his Public Service Company of Northern Illinois, Budd took on that job, too, as well as a continuing series of special assignments for the utilities tycoon.

By the end of 1917 the Insull management had spent over a million dollars for improvements to the North Shore. Several new steel or concrete bridges were constructed to replace wood structures, new rail and ballast were laid, 65,000 ties were replaced, and an extensive track resurfacing program started. Two new automatic substations, and new feeders, were installed to improve the railway's power distribution. A number of new stations and other buildings were constructed, and others were rebuilt. An extensive highway crossing signal program was started on 33 miles of line.

Passenger service was substantially improved in the first 18 months of Insull operation. The North Shore, which had received its first 15 steel passenger cars in 1915, purchased another 15 from the Jewett Car Company in 1917. By February 1917, when the new equipment was placed in service, the North Shore was operating a total of 30 high speed limited trains daily between Evanston and Milwaukee.

Among the new cars were three splendid combination parlor-dining cars, which were placed on limited runs, where they were operated as full diners on noon and evening runs, and as parlor cars at other times during the day.

Interiors of the parlor-dining cars were finished in mahogany and were furnished with comfortable arm chairs and detachable mahogany dining tables, which could be stored in special lockers when the cars were not in use as diners. Passengers were served from a complete menu and the service was claimed to be "comparable in every way with that enjoyed on steam road diners." Among limited trains employing the new equipment was a new noon diner train, the *Gold Coast Limited,* which was placed in operation on March 31, 1917. Normally made up of two coaches and one of the parlor-dining cars, the new train carried a special illuminated drumhead sign on the rear car.

In addition to their regular runs, the handsome new parlor-diners were frequently employed on special trains. Among the many dignitaries who traveled aboard the new cars to visit the vast Great Lakes Naval Training Station during 1918 were included Secretary of the Navy Josephus Daniels and Secretary of the Treasury William G. McAdoo.

Among other passengers traffic innovations of the new North Shore management were special tours to the lake region west of Milwaukee in conjunction with the Milwaukee Electric Railway &

Light Company, and to the west Michigan resort region in connection with the Pere Marquette Railway's Lake Michigan steamship service between Milwaukee and Ludington. Late in 1917 the North Shore even announced plans for a new sleeping car service between Chicago and Milwaukee. Sleeping cars would depart from each city at 10 p.m., it was announced, and passengers would be allowed to remain in their berths until 7 a.m. the following morning. The company evidently thought better of the idea, however, and the service was never actually begun.

By the end of the first full year under Insull management North Shore business had almost doubled. During 1915 the interurban had transported fewer than seven million passengers and earned total operating revenues of not quite a million dollars. In 1917 annual passenger traffic exceeded ten million passengers and operating revenues totaled over $1.7 million. By 1918 the North Shore was transporting almost 12 million passengers annually and earning gross revenues of almost $2.9 million. Contributing much of the increased traffic were the huge military training stations along the line. The Naval Training Station at Great Lakes had as many as 40,000 men at times, and such occasions as public reviews by the "jackies" drew crowds of as many as 30,000 to Great Lakes.

The *Gold Coast Limited* of 1917 provided the North Shore's first full dining car service. DONALD DUKE COLLECTION The exceptional elegance of the *Limited's* dining car is evident in this interior view of No. 406, one of three splendid all-steel parlor-dining cars received in 1917. A Santa Fe dining car chef and a crew of experienced waiters were hired to staff the new cars. ARTHUR D. DUBIN COLLECTION The North Shore's new Milwaukee passenger station, shown on the right, had three stub tracks, each with a capacity of five cars. DONALD DUKE COLLECTION

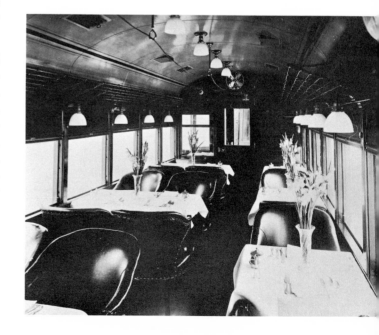

In 1918 the North Shore provided equipment for an unusual Navy recruiting train which operated from Great Lakes throughout the Central West over both interurban and steam railroads. Three flat cars were rigged to represent a U-boat chaser, a destroyer, and a submarine, and each car was equipped with a small cannon with which the recruiters announced their arrival along the line. A "jackie" band, part of the famous John Phillips Sousa organization at Great Lakes, accompanied the train.

To keep pace with the growing traffic the Insull management continued its massive improvement program, spending from half a million to a million dollars annually on additions and betterments to the property. More new passenger stations, power substations, and other structures were constructed. Large scale tie replacement, reballasting, and track resurfacing work were continued, and, in 1918, a program for replacement of 65 pound rail with 80 pound sections was begun. Some 250 tons of the heavier rail were laid in 1918 alone.

On August 6, 1919, the North Shore's long-cherished ambition to operate a true through service between Chicago and Milwaukee became a reality when interurban trains began operating directly into the Chicago Loop over the Northwestern Elevated Railroad. Early the next year the railway opened a splendid new Chicago passenger terminal at Adams Street and Wabash Avenue on the Loop. The first floor of the terminal was opulently decorated in Louis XV style. The lower walls were provided with a green marble finish, above which were installed panels of old rose imitation damask silk with gold rococo borders. Pilasters were of imitation Tennessee marble with Ionic columns and gilded caps. Green cathedral glass was installed around window openings in the ticket booths. The terminal restaurant was similarly decorated, with the addition of a domed sky blue ceiling with a skylight from which hung a white trellis, decorated with imitation green leaves.

Later in 1920 the company opened a handsome new terminal of almost equal elegance at Sixth and Sycamore (now Michigan) Streets in Milwaukee. Built at a cost of $600,000, the new structure was said to be, with considerable exaggeration, the largest electric railway terminal in the United States. The elaborate festivities that attended the opening of the terminal on September 15, 1920, were in marked contrast to the almost total lack of ceremony that had marked the opening of the line itself some 12 years previous. Milwaukee guests of the company, which included Mayor Hoan and other local dignitaries, were entertained at a luncheon at the Milwaukee Athletic Club, after which they inspected the new terminal. Accompanying President Budd aboard a special train from Chicago, which arrived in time for the dedication ceremonies, were Chicago Mayor Thompson and many other dignitaries, among them the presidents of the rival Chicago & North Western and Milwaukee Road.

Opened with elaborate ceremony on September 15, 1920, the North Shore's new Milwaukee terminal provided the railway with adequate facilities at the northern end of its line for the first time. The spacious passenger waiting room included a complete restaurant and soda fountain. Ample off-street loading and unloading space was provided for the railway's new freight pick up and delivery truck service. BOTH DONALD DUKE COLLECTION Included in the new Milwaukee terminal was this large freight house for the North Shore's rapidly growing merchandise despatch service. Sufficient track space for 14 merchandise cars was available.

Early in 1920 the North Shore's fleet of heavy steel cars was doubled in size with the delivery of 30 new interurbans from the Cincinnati Car Company as part of a record $800,000 new equipment order. Fifteen of the new cars were trailers, while 15 were motorized. The latter were equipped with four, 140 HP motors each and were capable of 80 m.p.h. top speeds. Among these new cars were two more parlor-dining cars for the company's increasingly popular luxury service, which permitted expansion of dining car service to three trains daily in each direction.

By mid-1920 the North Shore was operating a total of 160 daily trains, including 44 daily limited trains between Chicago and Milwaukee. The crack new *Badger Limited,* which went into service simultaneously with the opening of the new Milwaukee terminal, raced between the two cities on a schedule allowing only 2 hours 15 minutes for the journey. Stops were made only at Racine and Kenosha.

On February 15, 1922, the company's Chicago-Milwaukee limited train service was extended over the South Side Elevated Railroad to a terminal at 63rd and Dorchester on Chicago's South Side. Through service to and from Milwaukee was provided on an hourly basis. On the same date the North Shore introduced its new *Eastern Limited,* which offered close connections at Chicago in both directions with the *Broadway, Twentieth Century,* and *Capitol* limiteds for New York, Washington, and other eastern points. North Shore ticket agents made reservations on the steam road limiteds and "same train" through baggage checking was available. *Twentieth Century* passengers transferred directly at the LaSalle Street station, while special taxis transported *Broadway* passengers to Union Station from the Wells and Quincy elevated station. Stopping only at Racine and Kenosha, the *Eastern*

Beginning with an order for 30 new steel cars in 1920, the Cincinnati Car Company became one of the North Shore's principal car suppliers. The interior of No. 170 clearly shows the coal-fired stove used for hot water heating that was standard on all equipment. Seats in the smoking compartment were upholstered in imitation leather, while those in the main compartment were covered with green plush. O. F. LEE COLLECTION The exterior of No. 170 differed little from the original steel car design of 1915. DONALD DUKE COLLECTION

Limited operated on a 2 hour 10 minute schedule. Soon afterward the connecting Milwaukee Northern Railway and Milwaukee Electric Lines installed new parlor car limited services which made close connections at Milwaukee with the *Eastern Limited* for passengers from points as far distant as Sheboygan and Watertown.

Reconstruction of the North Shore's physical plant continued at the same rapid pace. Still more new stations, substations, and other structures were built. Additional highway crossing protection was provided, and block signals were installed on several sections of the line. Miles of trolley overhead and track were rebuilt. In 1921 the North Shore began using 100 pound rail for its new rail program, and during the next two years the heavier rail was provided in place of 65 pound rail on some 17 miles of track. By mid-1923 60 percent of the North Shore roadbed had been reballasted with crushed rock ballast.

Still more new equipment was ordered in 1922. Included in a 40-car order from the Cincinnati Car Company were another ten heavy steel interurbans for main line service. An unusual feature of these new cars was a thermostatically controlled dual electric and coal-fired hot water heating system. The electric heaters alone were employed during mild weather, while the hot water system was used during normal winter weather. In cases of extremely cold weather, both systems were placed in operation. To further assure passenger comfort, the cars were fitted with removable storm sash. During the summer screen windows were fitted in their place.

Among these new cars were included still another dining car and two splendid parlor-observation cars for the North Shore's extra fare limited train service. Delivered in July 1923, the new observation cars were furnished with large overstuffed mahogany lounge chairs, upholstered in a handsome, olive green figured plush. Arms of the chairs were arranged to hold a small tray for beverage or light lunch service, which was provided from a small kitchenette. The interiors were richly finished in mahogany, with an arched ceiling panelled in an "artistic manner." Green carpeting was laid on the floor. The open observation platforms were furnished with folding chairs, and were fitted with the traditional scalloped awning and brass railing. Names of the luxury limiteds on which the cars operated, which included the new *Prairie State Special* as well as the railway's crack *Eastern Limited,* were displayed on an illuminated drumhead sign.

Two more parlor-observation cars and another dining car were ordered the following year. So popular had become the North Shore's dining service that the combination parlor-dining cars previously operated could no longer satisfactorily handle the business, and the newest cars were built strictly as dining cars, with a seating capacity of 24. By 1925 the North Shore's dining cars were serving some 79,000 meals a year, and its parlor cars were transporting 39,000 extra fare passengers annually.

NORTH SHORE DRUMHEADS

An electric lighted drumhead sign was displayed on the rear of each North Shore name train. The sign was usually mounted on the brass-railed observation platform. The *Gold Coast Limited* of 1917 was North Shore's first name train. The *Eastern Limited* of 1922 offered close connection with steam railroad limiteds to and from the East. The *Prairie State Special* introduced in 1923 was a symbol of unsurpassable elegance.

North Shore luxury service attained new heights in 1923 with the delivery of two sumptuously furnished parlor-observation cars as part of a 40-car order from Cincinnati Car Company. No. 412, shown above, was one of two identical cars delivered the following year. ARTHUR D. DUBIN COLLECTION No. 416 was one of three new dining cars delivered in time for the 1926 opening of the Skokie Valley Route. Arranged as straight dining cars, the new units had a considerably greater seating capacity than older combination parlor-diner units. Although there was little evident difference from older equipment, aside from more attractive interior appointments, the new Cincinnati-built coaches shown in these exterior and interior views were provided with thermostatically controlled dual electric and coal-fired hot water heating systems, which permitted greatly improved control of car heating. O. F. LEE COLLECTION

Campaigning in the grand and traditional style, General Charles G. Dawes of Evanston, vice-presidential candidate on the Republican ticket with Calvin Coolidge rode a North Shore observation platform at Milwaukee in 1924. Dawes is the pipe smoking gentleman seated on the platform. O. F. LEE COLLECTION The last word in traction luxury of the 1920's was the North Shore's splendid new parlor-observation equipment, illustrated in the gallery on the opposite page. Fitted with polished brass railings, scalloped awnings, and drumhead signs, the elegant observation cars decorated the rear end of North Shore limiteds in the grand manner of the railway's steam road contemporaries. The crack *Interstate Limited* was displayed at the Wisconsin State Fair in 1927. TOP LEFT ARTHUR D. DUBIN COLLECTION — OPPOSITE VIEW — O. F. LEE COLLECTION.

Above, city car No. 360 waits for passengers at the end of the Glen Flora West line in Waukegan, adjacent to the North Shore's interurban main line. Below, a city car enroute to the main gate of the Great Lakes Naval Training Station emerges from the C&NW underpass at North Chicago Junction on the Shore Line Route. In the lower view is shown one of two city cars acquired from the Empire State Railways in 1918 and operated on North Shore's Waukegan local lines.

For the North Shore's several city car services the Insull management provided a modernization comparable to that for the company's interurban operations. Included in the North Shore's $800,000 new equipment order of 1919 were ten new single-truck Birney "safety cars," which were placed in operation on the company's Waukegan and North Chicago local lines. The operating economies afforded by the lightweight, one-man cars permitted North Shore to reduce headways from 15 minutes to eight minutes, and this increased frequency of service, together with reduced fares and the greater comfort of the new cars, brought a 39 percent increase in traffic carried by the city lines in less than a year. By 1923 traffic on the Waukegan and North Chicago city lines had reached 4.3 million passengers annually, compared to less than three million in 1919. Another dozen safety cars were ordered in 1922; and the introduction of improved one-man cars, reduced fares, and increased frequency of service on North Shore's Milwaukee city lines in February 1923, brought results comparable to those experienced in Waukegan and North Chicago. In the first three months of operation traffic increased by over 58 percent and revenues by 34 percent.

Early in the '20's the North Shore began an entry into bus operation. Originally, the company's bus service, according to North Shore President Budd, was intended to "keep others out," but the operation soon evolved into an important adjunct to the company's rail services. City bus services, planned to supplement streetcar lines, were operated in Waukegan and North Chicago. Extensive interurban motor coach services, operated from the North Shore communities to points as far distant as Lake Zurich, Woodstock, Fox Lake, and Antioch, Illinois, and Lake Geneva, Wisconsin, acted as feeder lines to the company's interurban rail lines. Special "parlor" coaches were available for charter service, which proved to be highly profitable. On one occasion a chartered North Shore parlor coach carried a YMCA glee club on an 1,870-mile tour to Pennsylvania and West Virginia.

The massive improvement program of the Insull management brought one record year after another for the North Shore. The system's passenger traffic was growing at an average rate of better than a million passengers annually, and between 1915 and 1923 the North Shore's annual passenger traffic increased from fewer than seven million to over 16 million passengers a year. During the same period the North Shore's gross operating revenues increased by over 550 percent, from less than a million dollars annually in 1915 to almost six million dollars in 1923.

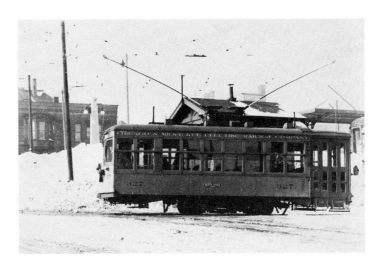

Lightweight, one-man Birney cars helped to rejuvenate North Shore local services in the early 1920's. At top, one of them lays over near the Milwaukee interurban terminal in the wake of a severe snow storm. Soon after World War I many interurban railways turned to new types of extremely lightweight cars as a means of combating rising operating costs. The North Shore was convinced that heavier, more luxurious, equipment was the answer to the growing competitive threat of private automobile ownership. Only once did the railway attempt the use of lightweight interurban equipment, with a 1923 order for two of the distinctive Cincinnati Car Company curved-side lightweights for operation on its Libertyville branch, shown in the two views to the right and below. Although their seating capacity was almost equal to that of the railway's standard steel cars, the lightweights weighed less than half as much. They were never popular on the North Shore and saw relatively little service before being displaced by the railway's standard heavy cars. CENTER AND BOTTOM—O. F. LEE COLLECTION

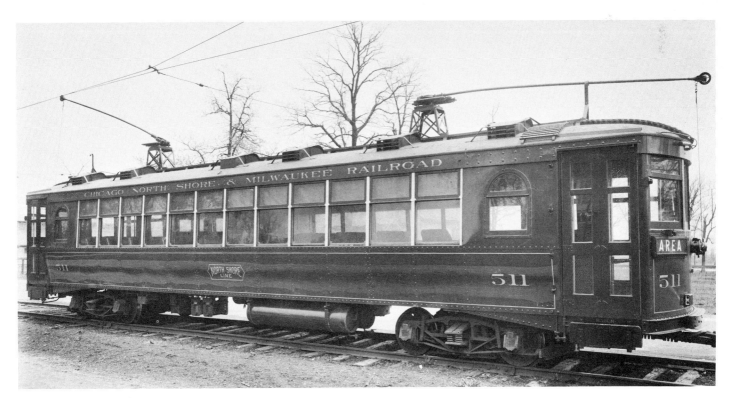

Jewett-built interurban No. 301 held down a Chicago local run as it paused at Kenilworth on the Shore Line Route in 1929. The older wooden cars built in 1909 for Evanston-Milwaukee limited trains had long since been downgraded to local service. O. F. LEE COLLECTION

The phenomenal achievements of the North Shore Line during seven years of Insull management won for the railway, in 1923, the first award of the Charles A. Coffin gold medal "for distinguished contribution to the development of electric transportation for the convenience of the public and the benefit of the industry."

The award had been established the year before by the board of directors of the General Electric Company in honor of the retirement of Charles A. Coffin, one of the founders and a former president of the company. A sum of $400,000 was set aside, to be known as the "Charles A. Coffin Foundation;" and annual income from the fund was to be devoted to encouraging and rewarding service in the electrical industry.

Selection of the North Shore to receive the Foundation's first annual electric railway award was made by a committee of the American Electric Railway Association, which unanimously chose the railway following examination of the "briefs" submitted by 17 competing electric railways. The gold medal and a $1000 contribution to the company's Employees' Mutual Benefit Association were presented to the North Shore on October 11, 1923, at the Association's Atlantic City convention.

Early in the 1920's the North Shore was quick to make use of the motor coach as a means of supplementing its interurban and local rail services. Above, motor coaches are lined up at the railway's Kenosha, Wisconsin, station for the evening rush. DONALD DUKE COLLECTION On the opposite page, a new White Motor Coach offers free rides to call attention to the new passenger connection. WHITE MOTOR COMPANY The Charles A. Coffin Medal awarded to the North Shore Line in 1923 is shown in the lower view. WILLIAM D. MIDDLETON COLLECTION

Along with the seemingly limitless capital applied to the massive physical transformation of the railway, Sam Insull brought with him to the North Shore a set of business principles that had been evolved in a quarter century of public utility operation. Far advanced for their time, these Insull principles had played no small part in the phenomenal growth of his utilities empire, and they would prove no less important in the spectacular success of the North Shore.

Foremost among these principles, from a human relations point of view at least, was a strong emphasis on safety, a subject which then often received little attention in the railroad industry. A vigorous North Shore safety program was established in 1917; and in only a year's time employee accidents had been reduced by 34 percent, personal injury and property damage accidents by 45 percent, and accident costs by a remarkable 62 percent, despite a 60 percent increase in the company's traffic. Within five years the North Shore had decreased its accident costs to less than a third of the average for the entire electric railway industry.

Among the many imaginative ideas applied to the North Shore's safety program was the "safety car," a converted passenger car which periodically traveled over the system acting as a mobile safety lecture room. Track laborers were picked up wherever they were found; and the car was run into the nearest siding, where a short safety meeting was conducted. The men were then returned to their place of work and the car continued on its way to pick up a fresh audience. Another unusual North Shore safety idea was the "butterfly," a sealed envelope containing a message warning of the dangers of death or injury from high speed cars, which motormen were instructed to throw to persons spotted trespassing on the company's right-of-way.

Still other North Shore safety innovations included the training of highly skilled first aid teams, and an active participation in school and community safety activities along its lines. During one four-and-a-half month period alone North Shore safety men delivered 570 lectures to a total of 22,548 public and parochial school pupils. Safety suggestions were actively sought from the company's employees, and more than 2,500 of them, almost all of which were found usable, were received in only five years. Several hundred thousand dollars a year was spent for the installation and maintenance of highway crossing protection and safety signs along the North Shore right-of-way.

Another Insull principle applied on the North Shore was that of enlightened labor relations. In 1921 the company organized an "Employees' Mutual Benefit Association," which provided liberal sick and death benefits. Employee members paid a dollar a month, to which the company added a contribution of 50 cents monthly per member. The North Shore assisted home building employees by furnishing free plans and specifications, cost estimates, and expert

43

I can save
a couple of days
in a *couple of hours*
Never mind the
letter, *I'll take the*
NORTH SHORE LINE

AUTUMN WOODS
NORTH SHORE LINE

GREEN BAY TRAIL
BY THE NORTH SHORE LINE

construction advice. The company encouraged a wide range of employee athletic and social activities, and sponsored an annual "reunion" for employees and their families, which extended from noon until midnight, so that everyone could attend. An orchestra and professional entertainers were engaged, and the railway served both a turkey dinner at noon and an evening supper.

The North Shore sponsored a broad educational program for its employees, which included everything from public speaking classes, to lectures on public utility operations, to company sharing of tuition costs for university extension courses. An unusual feature of the North Shore educational program was the company's "Americanization" classes. Finding that some 78 percent of its track laborers were foreign-born non-citizens, many of them illiterate, the company sponsored classes in both English and the requirements of American citizenship.

Merchandising, advertising, and public relations were highly polished arts among all of the Insull companies, but few of them could equal the North Shore Line's aggressive efforts in these directions. Literally no stone was left unturned by North Shore traffic men in their efforts to promote the company's passenger business. Department store information bureaus, steam railroad travel offices, and even hotel clerks and porters, were kept well informed about North Shore services. On one occasion the railway's traffic department provided a special motor coach tour through the Wisconsin lake country for personnel of various Chicago resort and information bureaus. By personal contact with organizations

Distinguished posters such as these, the work of prominent Chicago artists were a widely acclaimed part of the North Shore's extensive publicity campaign. Other posters illustrated the attractions that could be found on the North Shore Line.
CHICAGO HISTORICAL SOCIETY

planning convention trips, North Shore traffic solicitors succeeded in signing up some 6,000 people in one year alone for side trips from Chicago to the Wisconsin lake country via North Shore trains and motor coaches.

The company's charter car business was energetically promoted among lodges, fraternal societies, athletic groups, schools, and other organizations, and the North Shore usually operated several hundred such special trips every year. Chartered North Shore cars frequently operated to points on connecting interurban railways or the Chicago elevated system, and a Milwaukee group once even traveled all the way to Rockford, Illinois, on a chartered North Shore train which operated via the Chicago elevated system and three connecting interurban lines. A popular feature of the North Shore charter service was the provision of a special illuminated sign mounted on the head end of a train, which bore the emblem of the lodge or other group chartering the trip.

Reproduced above are two examples of the joint advertising frequently employed by the three closely affiliated Insull interurbans at Chicago. Following their acquisition in 1925 and 1926, North Shore president Britton I. Budd headed the South Shore Line and the Chicago, Aurora & Elgin as well.

No improvement or innovation in North Shore service was introduced without appropriate publicity and ceremony. Such important events as the opening of a new station, the introduction of new equipment, or expansion of the company's services were usually celebrated with a formal dinner, to which public officials, businessmen, and newspapermen were invited. In 1925, when two new limited train services were established, their names—the *Northland* and *Metropolitan* limiteds—were chosen in a spirited contest among North Shore riders.

North Shore services were widely advertised by means of stereoptican slides shown in motion picture theatres; and in 1922 the company produced two travelogue type movies, "The Green Bay Trail" and "The Pace of Progress," featuring the company's passenger and merchandise despatch services, which were shown in hundreds of theatres in Chicago, Milwaukee, and other cities. A monthly magazine, the *North Shore Bulletin,* promoting the railway and its on-line communities, was widely distributed among passengers. During the holiday season North Shore trainmen handed out a company Christmas card to every passenger.

Artistic billboards and lithographed posters which were, and are, masterpieces of display advertising art were widely used by the North Shore Line. The company's handsome posters, which were the work of prominent Chicago artists, drew wide critical acclaim. A now famous billboard challenged, "Did you ever travel 80 miles an hour?" while another depicted an interurban train racing an airplane, to convey the idea of North Shore speed in unmistakable terms.

A few years later the company erected at a number of its stations seven-and-a-half foot imitation marble statues of a town crier carrying a bell and a scroll which bore the famous "Did you ever travel 80 miles an hour?" message of North Shore speed.

A variety of novel service innovations drew a wide interest to the North Shore. In 1922 a North Shore parlor car was experimentally equipped with radio equipment, which proved capable of picking up grand opera broadcasts at any point on the system, and of transmitting by radio-telephone to points as far away as 15 miles. A variation of this idea was tried out a few years later, when phonographs were installed aboard two parlor-observation cars. Passengers were able to choose musical selections ranging from classical works to those of such popular artists as Paul Whiteman and Isham Jones. During the 1922 opera season in Chicago the railway attracted wide notice with its *Grand Opera Special*, which operated from Milwaukee direct to Congress and Wabash in Chicago, where a special canopy was erected between the elevated station and the

Probably no other advertisement was ever as successful in conveying the message of railroad speed as this famous North Shore billboard of the early 1920's. Imitation marble statues at several popular stations proclaimed the same message of North Shore speed. DONALD DUKE COLLECTION

Tedious operation through city streets, here illustrated by a five-car Waukegan-Chicago express on the long, slow drag down Greenleaf Avenue in Wilmette, always plagued the North Shore's original Evanston-Waukegan main line. Although right-of-way was acquired for a Wilmette bypass, the work was never carried out. JOHN STERN

entrance to the Auditorium Theatre so that opera-goers were protected from the weather. The special train included a dining car which served dinner during the southbound journey and a light supper on the return trip.

Still another Insull practice applied on the North Shore was the promotion of widespread public ownership of the company's stock. The company first began extensive sale of its securities to employees and the general public in 1923. By 1925 there were 8,250 North Shore stockholders and by 1926, when the company's stock was paying dividends of six to seven percent, there were more than 10,000 North Shore "owners."

By 1924, when its passenger traffic had reached almost three times the 1915 level, the North Shore Line was faced with a problem of increasingly serious proportions. The company's northern extension from Waukegan to Milwaukee, built between 1904 and 1908, had originally been constructed to exceptionally high standards and, with the extensive improvements to track, structures, and power distribu-

tion initiated by the Insull management, was more than adequate to accommodate the tremendous growth in high speed traffic. The original Chicago & Milwaukee route through the communities along the Lake Michigan shore between Waukegan and Evanston, however, was something else again.

While a number of improvements had been made at various times, this older "shore line" route still involved extended operation through city streets. The severe speed restrictions imposed by local communities, together with the generally poor standards of grade and curvature on the line, presented an almost insurmountable obstacle to any effort by the North Shore to further accelerate its Chicago-Milwaukee through schedules. Local traffic on the route, moreover, was substantially heavier than that on the system north of Waukegan, and by 1924 traffic on the double track route had almost reached the saturation point. Still another serious liability imposed by the route was the railway's inability, because of franchise restrictions, to operate carload freight service south of Highland Park.

One possible solution to the North Shore's dilemma was to completely reconstruct the line to high standards on a grade-separated elevated or depressed roadbed. The high costs and difficulties of carrying out this work in the heavily built-up lake shore communities, in addition to the costly temporary line that would be required while the work was in progress, raised the estimated cost for the project to an impossibly high level. Furthermore, the North Shore believed that continued traffic growth would ultimately require expansion of the route to four tracks in order to permit segregation of local and through traffic, a project that would be almost entirely out of the question in view of the extremely high property values prevailing in the "gold coast" communities along the lake shore, and the many other difficulties that would be encountered.

An attractive alternative to reconstruction of the shore line route was the construction of an entirely new high speed cut-off through the Skokie Valley several miles to the west of the original route. Such a line could be built at relatively low cost through open country where few construction difficulties would be encountered. With foresight typical of the Insull interests, this possibility had been anticipated several years earlier when the Insull-controlled Public Service Company of Northern Illinois had constructed a new high tension transmission line through the Skokie Valley to Waukegan. Between Niles Center, about six miles west of the old North Shore line at Evanston, and an intersection with the North Shore's Libertyville branch about a mile west of the old line at Lake Bluff, the power company had acquired for its transmission line a right-of-way

suitable for later construction of an electric railway. While the 23-mile cut-off that could be constructed over this route would be almost three miles longer than the old route, it would allow unrestricted high speed operation and would permit substantial reductions in Chicago-Milwaukee schedules.

Construction of a cut-off through the Skokie Valley offered several additional benefits as well. Although largely undeveloped, the Valley was in the natural path of Chicago suburban growth; and it was anticipated that the availability of fast electric transportation would encourage rapid development of the area, and consequently of North Shore commuter traffic. The new line would also provide a more direct outlet for the North Shore's Libertyville branch, and it would permit a greatly expanded North Shore freight business.

North Shore engineers estimated that the new high speed cut-off could be built for less than the cost of the temporary trackage alone that would be required for reconstruction of the original lake shore route. Accordingly, the Insull management decided to proceed with construction of the Skokie Valley cut-off, and in 1924 organized the subsidiary Chicago North Shore & Northern Railroad to carry out the project.

Construction of a five-mile section of the double track cut-off, extending to Niles Center from a junction with the old route at the Howard Street elevated station, was begun on April 4, 1924, and was carried to completion in less than ten months. This initial Niles Center extension included some of the most difficult construction problems encountered on

The high construction standards employed on the Skokie Valley Route are evident in these photographs taken shortly before opening of the line in June 1926. Visible in the top view is the method by which alternate catenary bridges were supported at one end by the transmission line towers previously installed on the right-of-way. ARTHUR D. DUBIN COLLECTION In sections which did not follow the transmission line, overhead bridge and catenary construction resembled mainline railroad electrification. DONALD DUKE COLLECTION The lower view illustrates one of nine stations of Spanish architecture constructed to accommodate the anticipated suburban traffic along the new route. Living quarters for agents were incorporated into the structures. ARTHUR D. DUBIN COLLECTION On the opposite page, a typical scene along the North Shore's original Shore Line Route illustrates the marked difference in standards between this line and the splendid new route through the Skokie Valley. ARA MESROBIAN

This massive steel structure which carried the Niles Center extension over a street, two railroads and a drainage canal, was the largest single structure on the entire 23-mile bypass through the Skokie Valley. WILLIAM D. MIDDLETON The imposing structure at Asbury Avenue was typical of the stations on the five-mile Niles Center Division, the first section of the Skokie line to be completed. ARTHUR D. DUBIN COLLECTION Official opening of the Niles Center Division was marked by this gala celebration at the Dempster Street station on March 28, 1925. Service was operated by the Chicago Rapid Transit Company, which leased trackage rights from the North Shore. O. F. LEE COLLECTION

the entire Skokie Valley route. In order to maintain a largely grade-separated route, extensive cut and fill work were required. A concrete subway, which carried the line under the main line tracks of the Chicago & North Western Railroad, had to be constructed without interruption to traffic on the steam railroad; and a total of seven steel and concrete bridges were built for grade separations at streets or other railroads. The largest of these was a structure totaling 1,000 feet in length and made up of steel plate girders and deck trusses spanning as much as 120 feet, which carried the electric line over the Chicago & West Ridge Railroad, a channel of the Chicago drainage canal, and a Chicago & North Western branch. Supporting structures for bridges, and other right-of-way installations were constructed to accommodate later expansion of the route to four tracks.

A new 2,000-KW automatic substation was constructed to supply power to the new line, and a third rail power distribution system was installed on most of the route. West of Crawford Avenue-Prairie Road, where the line was located at street level, a catenary trolley system, supported by steel bridges, was installed.

The eight ornately finished stations on the extension were built to unusually high standards. Reinforced concrete and brick were extensively used in their construction, and they were provided with concrete high level platforms and canopies. White cast stone and terra cotta were used for exterior trim. Floors were of terrazzo or pink marble, and interior walls were of brick or pink Tennessee art marble.

Passenger service over the new line between Howard Street and Niles Center was opened on February 1, 1925, by the Chicago Rapid Transit Company, which had leased trackage rights from the North Shore. Operation of North Shore trains was not contemplated until completion of the entire cut-off.

Construction of the remaining 18-mile section of the cut-off between Niles Center and a junction with the Libertyville branch was begun in June 1925, and was rushed to completion in only a year's time. At the height of the construction effort during the spring of 1926 as many as 1,500 men were engaged in the work at one time; and crews worked day and night, seven days a week, in order to complete the project on schedule. A huge construction camp, capable of housing and feeding a thousand men, was set up at Blodgett (now Briergate) to accommodate a large part of the work force.

The standards employed in construction of the final section of the Skokie Valley line were among the highest ever used by an interurban railway. There were no towns at all north of Niles Center, and only a few grade crossings, and the level terrain permitted construction of the line on virtually tangent track. The 135 foot right-of-way employed for the cut-off was sufficient not only for a future total of four high speed tracks, but for two transmission tower lines, 10 to 12 power pole lines, high pressure gas mains, and other utility services as, well. The maximum grade on the line was only 0.5 percent; and all curves were superelevated for a maximum speed of 70 m.p.h., with the exception of the curve joining the new line with the Libertyville branch, where speeds were restricted to 55 m.p.h.

The 48 miles of new track constructed required over 8,000 tons of rail and more than 165,000 ties; and a total of 88,000 cubic yards of crushed stone and gravel ballast was furnished from the North Shore's Libertyville quarry for the work. Initially, the line was laid with 80 pound rail on plain white oak ties. After settlement and consolidation of the roadbed under traffic for one season, these were to be replaced with 100 pound rail and creosoted red oak ties.

Power was supplied to the final section of the cut-off from five new automatic rotary converter or mercury-arc rectifier substations, which were constructed at four-mile intervals. A compound catenary overhead distribution system, requiring 138 miles of wire, was installed. The catenary system was supported by 469 catenary bridges, comprising 1,200 tons of steel, located at spacings of 250 or 300 feet. On much of the line the railway was able to use the Public Service Company's transmission line towers, which were spaced at 500 feet, to support one end of alternate catenary bridges.

Three interlocking plants were required on the final section of the cut-off. A 24-lever mechanical plant was installed south of Dempster Street at the junction with the Niles Center extension; a 31-lever all-electric plant was installed at Skokie Junction, where the Chicago & North Western's Lake Bluff branch was crossed at grade; and a 55-lever all-electric plant was installed at South Upton, where the new line intersected the Libertyville branch.

Anticipating a greatly increased traffic over the Libertyville branch following completion of the Skokie Valley Route, the North Shore completed double tracking of the last three miles of the branch between Libertyville and its Mundelein terminal, and constructed a handsome new station at Munde-

lein in the "standard" North Shore design of tapestry brick with white stone trim and a green tile roof.

Construction of the new line had set off what was described as a "spectacular real estate boom" in the Skokie Valley, and property values quickly increased by as much as eight or ten times. The North Shore's indefatiguable publicity organization lost no opportunity to publicize the new suburban territory. Nine attractive new stations of Spanish architecture were constructed to accommodate the anticipated Skokie Valley commuter traffic, and over 75,000 people competed for $1,000 in prizes offered by the North Shore in a contest to name the new stations.

The opening of service over the new line on June 5, 1926, was celebrated amid great fanfare and expressions of confidence in a golden future. Said President Budd, "The Skokie Valley Route of the North Shore Line represents an investment of $10,000,000 in the future of the comparatively undeveloped North Shore region lying to the west of the territory now served by our Shore Line Route. We have made this big investment, secure in our confidence that this region is destined to become one of Chicago's most beautiful and desirable residential districts. We have every reason to believe that our confidence is not misplaced."

Simultaneous with the construction of its high speed cut-off through the Skokie Valley the North Shore completed double-tracking of the Libertyville branch to its terminal at Mundelein where this handsome new station was constructed. ARTHUR D. DUBIN COLLECTION Below, a three-car *Milwaukee Limited* races through Dempster Street station, five miles west of Howard Street. From 1925 until 1948 Chicago Rapid Transit shuttle trains operated here from Howard Street. Following the North Shore's 1963 abandonment the Chicago Transit Authority bought the track and restored "L" service to Dempster Street. O. F. LEE COLLECTION

The Cincinnati Car Company delivered 20 new steel interurban coaches and three dining cars in time for the inauguration of service over the new line. Running times for Chicago-Milwaukee trains were reduced by as much as 25 minutes, and a new hourly service was installed on the branch to Libertyville and Mundelein. Coincident with the opening of the new service, the North Shore reduced its commuter fares by as much as 50 percent.

Opening of the Skokie Valley Route highlighted one of the greatest years in the North Shore Line's entire history. Gross operating revenues for 1926 reached a new high of almost $7.6 million; and the railway transported a total of almost 19.5 million passengers, a figure that would not be exceeded for almost 20 years.

In 1928 the Pullman Car & Manufacturing Company delivered an order of 18 new interurban cars of exceptionally luxurious interior appointments. Car No. 746, shown below, was one of 15 coaches seating 50 passengers in individual bucket seats. Two dining cars and a parlor-observation car included in the order afforded standards of luxury and decor equal in every respect to those of the finest contemporary steam railroad equipment. All three cars were finished in walnut interior paneling and were provided with black and gold patterned carpeting. All of the new cars were finished in the North Shore's new orange and maroon exterior color scheme. ALL, O. F. LEE COLLECTION

Greatly influencing the North Shore's timing of the Skokie Valley Route construction and the record speed with which the work was carried out were the plans for the great 28th International Eucharistic Congress of the Catholic Church, which was to be held at Chicago during June 1926. The closing exercises of the Congress were to be held at St. Mary of the Lake Seminary in Mundelein on June 24; and it was anticipated that a crowd of a million people, believed to be the greatest assemblage of people for a single event in world history, would attend the ceremonies. Completion of the Skokie Valley Route in time for the Congress would place the North Shore Line in a position to accommodate a major share of this traffic.

Engineers who studied the gigantic transportation problem for more than a year prior to the event estimated that about 275,000 of the huge crowd would travel from Chicago to Mundelein by rail, with by far the greatest share of the load to be carried by the North Shore Line and the Chicago Rapid Transit Company. In order to route the traffic according to the ability of the several railroads to accommodate it, Chicago was subdivided into districts and visitors to the ceremonies were required to travel according to set rules. An estimated 15,000 could travel directly to Mundelein on the Soo Line, and another 30,000 to Libertyville on the Milwaukee Road. The Chicago & North Western could transport an estimated 60,000 people to Lake Bluff, where they would transfer to special North Shore shuttle trains. The Rapid Transit lines and the North Shore would have to accommodate the remaining 170,000 people, in addition to the 60,000 that would have to be shuttled between Lake Bluff and Mundelein and those traveling from Wisconsin and other North

Shore points north of Chicago. To do the job it was estimated that a six-car train would have to leave the Chicago Loop every two minutes during an eight-hour period beginning at daybreak, and that shuttle trains would have to operate from Lake Bluff every three minutes.

A total of 932 Chicago Rapid Transit cars were to be operated in the service from the Loop directly to Mundelein over the Skokie Valley line. Many of these cars had to be specially equipped with trolley poles for this purpose. North Shore Line equipment was to be used to operate the 13 eight-car trains required for the Lake Bluff-Mundelein shuttle service and to accommodate visitors traveling to the Congress from North Shore points between Evanston and Milwaukee.

Two temporary 400 foot platforms were constructed at Lake Bluff, where Chicago & North Western passengers transferred to the shuttle trains. On a ten acre site opposite the Seminary gates at Mundelein the North Shore constructed a temporary, six-track stub terminal with a total capacity

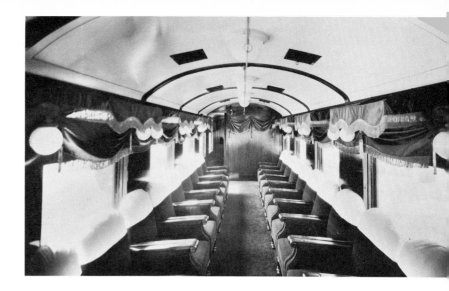

On the left is shown the elaborate temporary facilities installed by the Chicago Rapid Transit and the North Shore at Mundelein to accommodate the crowds attending the Eucharistic Congress. In the foreground is one of the two complete hospital units provided for first aid purposes. Hospital car No. 2756 was originally built as a deluxe funeral car for the Metropolitan West Side Elevated. The tents in the background provided space for 25 beds. WILLIAM D. MIDDLETON COLLECTION Loading chutes helped control the tremendous crowds. Cardinal Bonzano, the papal legate to the Congress, nine assisting cardinals, and other members of the church hierarchy traveled to the Seminary grounds aboard the heavily decorated special five-car train shown below. ARTHUR D. DUBIN COLLECTION The interior of the train's parlor-observation car was fitted with special hangings in the papal colors. O. F. LEE COLLECTION

of 52 cars, which would permit simultaneous loading or unloading of six trains of six to eight cars each. In order to control the tremendous crowds anticipated for the return movement, a loading chute with a capacity of 1,000 people was constructed at the head of each platform. Passengers entered the chutes from a "stockade" which had a capacity of some 9,000 people, or about 18 to 20 trainloads. Train movements were directed from an overhead bridge across the loading tracks.

To help feed the crowd the North Shore constructed a temporary lunch stand which had 200 feet of counter space and was operated by a kitchen force of 200. Two complete hospitals, each consisting of a hospital car and tents with a capacity of 25 beds, were provided by the North Shore and the Chicago Rapid Transit. In order to reduce the sudden rush on its facilities by homeward-bound passengers, the North Shore made provision for band concerts and motion pictures to entertain the crowd at the conclusion of the ceremonies.

Altogether, the North Shore and the Rapid

Transit spent some $150,000 on the special facilities and equipment required for the movement. These thorough preparations, and the careful planning that went into the operation, permitted the two electric lines to handle the unprecedented traffic with remarkably little difficulty.

After the papal legate, Cardinal Bonzano, and his assisting cardinals had been transported to the Seminary aboard a heavily festooned *Cardinals' Special* decorated in the papal colors, the business of moving the crowds began in earnest. For eight consecutive hours a loaded train arrived at Mundelein on an average of every 40 seconds, and by 10 a.m. an estimated 130,000 passengers had been discharged at the special Mundelein terminal.

The tensest moment of the day came early in the afternoon, when a severe rainstorm set off a violent rush to the North Shore terminal to catch homebound trains. Guard fences and gates were broken down, men and women lost their clothing, and many people fainted in the crush at the gates. Only heroic efforts by North Shore employees and Skokie construction forces held the crowd in check and finally restored order.

By the time the remarkable 18-hour, daybreak to midnight mass movement was over, some 820 trains, made up of 5,216 cars, had operated into or out of the Mundelein terminal; and the North Shore-Chicago Rapid Transit combination had transported a phenomenal total of 225,000 outbound and 275,000 inbound passengers. It was the greatest mass movement in interurban history, and the biggest day's traffic the three-week-old Skokie Valley Route would ever know. It was, as a Chicago newspaper described it, "a miracle in transportation," and the North Shore had carried it off without so much as a single mishap or injury to a passenger on its cars.

Six cars of Chicago-bound commuters hurry along the freshly ballasted right-of-way of the Skokie Valley Route. The high tension towers, latticework catenary bridges, compound catenary, and heavy rail and ballast of the Skokie line created an enduring image of the North Shore as the very model of a high-speed, *super interurban*. In the view at the upper right a Mundelein train makes a brief stop at Sheridan Elms. The station, shown in the view just below, was one of the handsome "Insull Spanish" structures erected at the time the line was opened in 1926. At the lower right a group of Chicago-bound commuters press forward as a five-car train rolls into the Dempster Street station, the last stop before Howard Street. ALL— DONALD DUKE

Even as construction crews pushed the new high-speed line north through the Skokie Valley, the North Shore's massive rehabilitation program for the remainder of the system continued at an undiminished pace. Over 30,000 new ties were installed yearly, more new 100 pound rail was laid, and by the end of 1925 fully 75 percent of the entire line had been provided with new crushed stone ballast. During 1926 the installation of automatic block signals was completed between North Chicago and Winthrop Harbor and within the next year was extended to the Wisconsin state line. In 1925, on the main line north of Lake Bluff, the North Shore began the replacement of simply suspended trolley wire supported by wood poles with a compound catenary system carried on steel bridges identical to that being installed on the new Skokie Valley Route. Ultimately, the company planned to extend the new overhead construction to the entire railway, and to convert from pole trolley to pantograph current collection.

Above, a Chicago-bound train off the Mundelein branch crosses the Chicago & North Western westside freight by-pass at the South Upton Junction interlocking tower. Below, a northbound train accelerates on third rail trackage just beyond the Howard Street station, where Skokie Valley Route trains left Chicago Transit Authority rails. Third rail operation extended to Crawford Avenue on the Niles Center section of the Skokie line. BOTH DONALD DUKE COLLECTION On the far right are shown two nighttime camera studies at Mundelein. Surrounded by darkened interurbans awaiting the morning rush back to the city, a late evening Chicago local waits for departure time. BOTH WILLIAM D. MIDDLETON

By the end of 1926 the massive investment of the Insull management had increased the total valuation of the railway almost three and a half times, from not quite $12.3 million in 1916 to more than $41.4 million. The railway owned some 256 miles of track, almost 200 passenger cars, over 50 mer-

chandise cars and locomotives, almost 250 pieces of freight and work equipment, and 47 motor coaches. Gross operating revenues were over six and a half times those of 1916, and net income was running in the vicinity of three quarters of a million dollars a year.

While the Insull-managed North Shore was doing very well indeed, things were going nowhere nearly as well elsewhere in the interurban railway industry. The rapid growth of private automobile ownership following World War I, together with the construction of a vast network of hard-surfaced roads, had brought increasingly difficult times for the industry. As operating revenues began to decline, there was a growing number of abandonments among the weaker companies. After reaching a peak of some 18,100 miles in 1917, U. S. interurban mileage began a steady decline; and within the next ten years over 1,700 miles of the U. S. interurban network had been abandoned.

By 1927 there were even a few troublesome signs on the North Shore. For the first time in over a decade of steady growth there was a slight decline in North Shore passenger traffic, although the loss in revenue was more than made up by an increase in freight traffic. Largely because of the heavy fixed charges resulting from the Skokie Valley Route con-

struction, North Shore's 1927 net income dropped below a half million dollars for the first time in six years. But these were minor problems, and no one could see anything but a golden future for the super-interurban. Said President Budd in 1927, "Well located interurban lines, instead of being obsolete, are in reality entering upon the period of their greatest usefulness."

There were several encouraging new innovations in North Shore passenger traffic. In 1927 the company began participating in interline ticketing with the steam railroads, and a year later North Shore agents began selling Pullman tickets to any point in the country. It was one of the few interurbans in the U. S. ever granted this privilege by the Pullman Company. In 1928 the North Shore began one of the first joint interurban-air line services. Agents at Milwaukee, Racine, and Kenosha sold joint rail-air tickets for air line services from Chicago to points throughout the Midwest and the East via Stout Air Lines, Universal Air Lines, and the Embry-Riddle Company. Passengers rode North Shore trains to 63rd Street in Chicago, where they transferred to surface cars which carried them directly to the hangars of the Chicago Municipal Airport at West 63rd and Cicero Avenue.

North Shore confidence in the future was re-

NORTH SHORE LINE
TO
MILWAUKEE

Ten unusually large and heavy city cars built by the St. Louis Car Company for the North Shore's Milwaukee and Waukegan local services were included in a $900,000 new equipment order in 1927. Above, one of them rolls down South 5th Street enroute to the Milwaukee local line's Oklahoma Avenue terminal. Below, another of the group climbs the hill past the North Shore's Milwaukee station. Visible beyond are the train shed and ornate tower of the Milwaukee Road station. GORDON E. LLOYD The poster reproduced at left matched an airplane against an interurban train to convey the message of North Shore speed. One Midwestern interurban actually staged such a race as a publicity stunt. CHICAGO HISTORICAL SOCIETY On the page at the right, a converted parlor-observation car heads a late afternoon commuter train on the Mundelein branch. JOHN GRUBER

flected late in 1927 by new equipment orders totaling $900,000, which included two new freight locomotives, ten plush upholstered lightweight city cars for the Waukegan and Milwaukee services, and 18 splendid new steel interurban cars from the Pullman Car & Manufacturing Company. Fifteen of the new interurbans were coaches, finished with mahogany interior trim, and seating 50 in individual bucket seats upholstered in gray Byzantine plush. The remainder of the order was made up of two dining cars and a parlor-observation car, which were provided with "modishly designed" interiors of buff colors, walnut paneling, and felt-padded black and gold carpeting. The 17 revolving easy chairs in the parlor-observation car were upholstered in a light blue frieze plush. All 18 of the new interurbans were finished in the North Shore's new orange and maroon color scheme, and one of the cars was experimentally equipped with Hyatt roller bearings. Only two years later another 25 interurban coaches were ordered from the Standard Steel Car Company for early 1930 delivery.

Both 1928 and 1929 were good years for the North Shore. Gross operating revenues continued to increase, exceeding $8 million for the first time in the company's history in 1929, and net income

climbed back up to around three quarters of a million annually. Despite the widening depression that followed the November 1929 stock market crash, the Insull super-interurban did reasonably well in 1930. Although gross revenues dropped by well over a million, operating costs went down, too; and the company had a comfortable net income of almost $600,000.

Then, in 1931, the bottom fell out. Operating revenues were down almost $3 million in only two years, salary cuts were ordered, dividends were suspended, and the North Shore ended the year with a net loss of almost $750,000. The next year was even worse. Revenues dropped to less than half the 1929 level; the annual loss approached $1.7 million; and by the end of September 1932, the North Shore, unable to pay its bills, followed much of the great Insull utilities empire into bankruptcy. Although Britton Budd would remain with the North Shore for another five years as a receiver, Sam Insull was forced to resign his board chairmanship, to begin the ignominious final chapter of his life.

Sam Insull was gone now, the great years were over, and the North Shore would never be the same again.

4

The Troubled Years

SKOKIE VALLEY ROUTE
MUNDELEIN

JOHN GRUBER

North Shore's busy South Upton tower not only controlled the four-way junction of the electric line's Lake Bluff-Mundelein branch with the Skokie Valley Route, but also protected the crossing of the Mundelein branch with the Chicago & North Western. Here a six-car rush hour train heels over as it rolls through the special track work before crossing the North Western line. JOHN GRUBER

The depression-induced North Shore bankruptcy of 1932 proved that Insull's interurban, too, was vulnerable to the forces that by 1933 had reduced the nation's interurban empire to little more than half its 1917 peak of over 18,000 miles; and the North Shore was to lead a troubled existence throughout much of the remaining three decades of its operation.

From its record loss of nearly $1.7 million in 1932, the North Shore began a painfully slow recovery. Losses in 1933 and 1934 exceeded a million and a quarter annually and continued at a lesser rate throughout the depression years.

Despite its financial troubles, the North Shore continued to display much of the zeal that had characterized the great Insull years. The railway's already remarkable high speed performance was steadily improved throughout the depression years, and reached the highest level in the company's entire history during the early 1940's. In 1936 North Shore engineers conducted a series of experiments to eliminate the tendency of trucks to "nose" at high speeds. As a result of the tests, a cylindrical wheel tread design, replacing the conventional conical tread, was developed. "So smooth than even a full cup of coffee won't spill," claimed the North Shore for its new "non-sway safety wheels."

Late in the 1930's the North Shore, together with the Chicago & North Western, the W.P.A., and the local communities involved, carried out an extensive grade separation project at Glencoe, Winnetka, and Kenilworth on its Shore Line Route. Nearly four miles long, the $3.5 million project eliminated over a dozen grade crossings as well as two stretches of operation through city streets. The highest possible standards were observed in construction of the relocation. Heavy rail and crushed stone ballast were employed in track construction, a compound catenary overhead system supported by steel structures was installed, and high level loading platforms were provided at the new stations.

A major crisis came in 1938, when deteriorating labor relations brought a paralyzing strike that shut down the railway for 51 days, and serious consideration was given to abandonment of the entire property. Instead, the North Shore, with a vigor that Sam Insull would have approved, elected to begin a valiant effort to regain its lost traffic.

Highlighting a dramatic North Shore program for passenger traffic recovery were two new streamlined *Electroliner* trains, which were ordered from the St. Louis Car Company in 1939 and placed in service early in 1941. Beginning in 1940, some 42 standard steel coaches and dining cars of the Insull era were extensively improved and refurbished for operation on both Chicago-Milwaukee limited trains and Shore Line Route suburban services. New seating and lighting were provided, heating and ventilating systems improved, and sound-reducing ceilings and rubber tiled floors installed.

World War II brought back, for a few brief years, a traffic level comparable to that of the great years of the 1920's. Total passenger traffic climbed steadily from barely ten million revenue passengers in 1940 to almost 28 million by 1945, and total operating revenues increased by almost 200 percent during the same period to reach a peak of nearly ten million dollars in 1945. Aided by wartime profits, which reached as much as a million dollars annually, the reorganized North Shore finally emerged from 14 years of bankruptcy in November 1946.

But trouble and crisis returned swiftly at war's end. Passenger traffic dropped precipitously to prewar levels and kept right on declining. Local streetcar services in Waukegan and North Chicago were converted to bus operation in 1947. Both LCL and "piggyback" freight services, which had declined rapidly after the war, were given up the same year.

Despite the adversities of the bankrupt depression years, the North Shore made some notable progress. One of the most significant achievements was the Winnetka grade separation project shown here. Shore Line Route trains began using it late in 1940. On the right is a view of the heavy steel overhead structure and catenary hangers. In the center, a view along the well built right-of-way, which employed heavy rail and crushed rock ballast. BOTH OHIO BRASS COMPANY In the lower scene two Shore Line trains pass along the new line which eliminated more than a dozen grade crossings at Winnetka. On the opposite page upper left, the by-pass is seen from the head-end of a northbound train. JOHN STERN While construction work was carried out, Shore Line trains operated temporarily over the adjacent Chicago & North Western rails. GORDON E. LLOYD At the bottom, track crews repair the heavily traveled C&NW rails following completion of the new North Shore by-pass. OHIO BRASS COMPANY

Throughout most of its history the North Shore enjoyed a close relationship with the U. S. Navy. In 1906 the railway joined with a group of Chicago area businessmen to contribute $150,000 for the purchase of a 168-acre tract at North Chicago, which was conveyed free to the government for construction of the Great Lakes Naval Training Station. For more than half a century thereafter the North Shore was the "Midwest sailors' favorite railroad". Countless Navymen rode North Shore trains on weekend liberties to Chicago and Milwaukee, or on their way to wartime action during two world wars and the Korean conflict. On this page sailors bound for weekend liberty flock aboard the electric cars. TOP LEFT AND RIGHT — JOHN GRUBER. ALL OTHERS OFFICIAL U. S. NAVY PHOTOGRAPHS On the opposite page a pair of Great Lakes whitehats prepares to board a Milwaukee-bound limited. WILLIAM D. MIDDLETON

Candid scenes photographed at the North Shore's Milwaukee terminal during the final years of operation. On the right, the hoof-nosed front end of an *Electroliner* was plastered with wet, sticky snow gathered during a 1960 blizzard. In the lower view a conductor checks his watch as departure time approaches, while opposite, two employees discuss matters of evident gravity at the end of the station platform. At the lower left, passengers crowd around the ticket window just before train time in the late evening. ALL JOHN GRUBER In the upper left the exterior of the terminal building as seen from Michigan Street facing west. DONALD DUKE

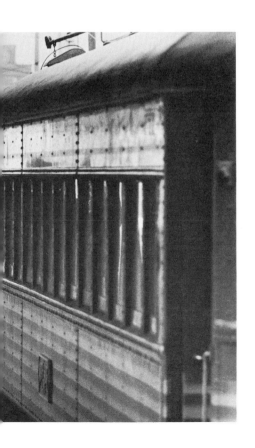

On a wet, misty night in July 1961, a pair of *Silverliners* in from Chicago wait for a green traffic light at South 6th and National in Milwaukee. RICHARD J. SOLOMON On the left, a switchtender ventures out into a snowy Milwaukee street to line the switches after a four-car Chicago-bound train leaves the terminal. On the opposite page, a northbound train approaches the end of the private right-of-way at Harrison Street in Milwaukee. BOTH JOHN GRUBER

In 1948 another prolonged strike, this one lasting more than three months, shut down the system; and only a better-than-40 percent commuter fare increase enabled the company to meet the resultant wage increases and resume operation. Dining car service, excepting tavern-lounge service on the *Electroliner* trains, was discontinued in 1949. Local streetcar service in Milwaukee was given up altogether in 1951.

Late in 1948 the company began a prolonged effort to abandon the commuter-heavy, chronically money-losing 37-mile Shore Line Route. After more than two years of hearings the company's initial abandonment petition was turned down by the Illinois Commerce Commission in 1951, but a renewed Shore Line abandonment effort was finally successful in mid-1955; and for a time it seemed that the remainder of the system had a promising future.

But barely three years later, in June 1958, the North Shore was back before the regulatory bodies again, this time citing a ten-year operating loss in excess of four million dollars, and asking for permission to abandon all operations. Setting some kind of record for governmental deliberations of their kind, the resulting proceedings dragged on intermittently for some four and a half years.

Clouding the issues as the North Shore fought for permission to end operation was its relation to Susquehanna Corporation, the Delaware holding company which owned the railroad. Founded in the illogic of U. S. tax law, Susquehanna originated with a voluntary North Shore reorganization in 1953, under which some five million dollars of North Shore assets were used to create the holding company. Assuming ownership of the North Shore and its several subsidiary bus operations, and diversifying into such activities as mining, uranium processing, chemicals, and electronics, Susquehanna had made a good thing out of writing off North Shore operating losses against its profits in other activities and stood to profit even more in the form of tax credits from the abandonment of the North Shore. One estimate placed the total gain at anywhere from $17 million to $28 million. Opponents to the abandonment charged, with understandable suspicion, that Susquehanna had no interest in keeping the North Shore going.

But all the controversy over Susquehanna Corporation, and the variety of other claims and charges advanced by opponents to the abandonment, served only to obscure the central fact that under the social and economic conditions prevailing in the 1960's the operation of North Shore passenger service as

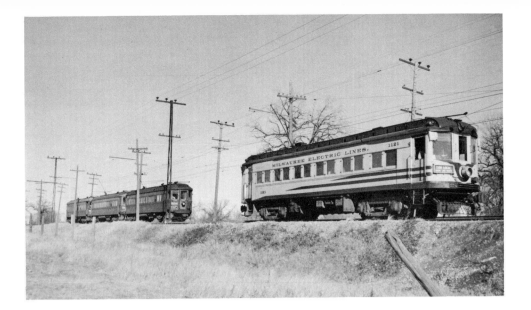

An early morning Chicago to Mundelein local train pounds across the Chicago & North Western westside freight line at South Upton tower. WILLIAM D. MIDDLETON The unlikely meet shown above took place in 1949 at Zion, Illinois, when an enthusiast organization chartered a Milwaukee Electric interurban for an outing on the North Shore. Until 1947 the Milwaukee Electric was a competitor for North Shore's Milwaukee-Racine-Kenosha traffic. GORDON E. LLOYD

Bridges of every description graced the North Shore right-of-way. Above, a Chicago-bound train rumbles onto the drainage canal bridge in the Skokie district. The extra wide concrete piers were so constructed to permit eventual expansion of the line to four tracks. On the right, this rustic trestle over the Des Plaines River just east of Libertyville on the Mundelein branch was a favorite spot for photographs. Here, a *Silverliner* forms a near-perfect reflection. BOTH WILLIAM D. MIDDLETON At the top of the opposite page a two-car *Silverliner* train minutes out of Milwaukee thunders over Chicago & North Western rails. DONALD DUKE COLLECTION

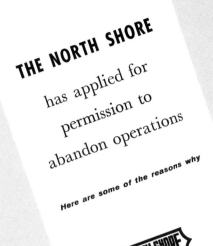

THE NORTH SHORE

has applied for permission to abandon operations

Here are some of the reasons why

NORTH SHORE LINE

In June 1958, the North Shore was before the regulatory bodies citing a ten-year operating loss in excess of four million dollars and asking permission to abandon all operations. Some of the reasons were set forth in this reproduced folder which was distributed to passengers and interested parties. DONALD DUKE COLLECTION

"Railroad passenger business, as presently conducted, is not and cannot be operated at a profit."

This comment by the New York Public Service Commission, one of the industry's major regulatory bodies, is a capsule statement of North Shore's reasons for seeking to abandon the line and its operations.

The short line interurban electric railway once was a widespread mode of passenger transportation in the United States. But when you except a few isolated instances—of which the North Shore is one—you find these lines have long since failed and disappeared from the scene, victims of changing times and changing transportation patterns.

Today it is an established fact that the railroad industry as a whole is in trouble. The railroads are seeking federal relief through legislation now before Congress. Commuter passenger business is recognized as a devastating factor in the railroads' illness. This is true of even the major lines that have substantial non-commuter revenues from which to subsidize their passenger operations. Even during the post-war period of general railroad prosperity, passenger business was a drain on railroad earnings. It had to be subsidized then, as now, by other operations.

It's not the commuter's fault; nor is it the railroads' fault. It's a combination of circumstances and the economic facts of life.

When you recognize that a great American industry finds commuter service a threat to its operating ability, you may find it easier to understand why the North Shore—a small and specialized segment of the industry, dependent on passenger traffic for some 80 per cent of its revenues—is forced to seek line abandonment.

Mass railway transportation of urban and suburban traffic no longer can be conducted by private enterprise with its limited amounts of capital. Time and again this has proved true elsewhere; now it is proving true right here at home. It has been acknowledged in major cities, including Chicago, with the establishment of public transportation systems such as the Chicago Transit Authority. It has been recognized in Illinois by the establishment of a legislative committee which even now numbers metropolitan transportation difficulties among the problems to which it seeks solutions.

And, of more immediacy to you and to us, it is being recognized by our filing of an abandonment petition with the Interstate Commerce Commission, the Illinois Commerce Commission and the Public Service Commission of Wisconsin. We have requested joint concurrent hearings by the three commissions and anticipate that they will be held in the near future.

Some reasons why

It would take a sizable brochure to relate and document the many factors that enter into the abandonment decision, but we would like to tell you some of the salient facts.

1) The North Shore is exhausting its cash resources. It has become overwhelmingly obvious that income from operations cannot sustain passenger service. We have reached the same impasse that brought dissolution to the many other short line passenger operations that failed in other metropolitan areas.

2) Since World War II the North Shore has sustained losses and declines in cash funds year after year. At the same time we have made substantial capital outlays, many of them by order of railroad regulatory bodies, to maintain the safety and dependability of operations. It probably has been obvious to you that North Shore's limited maintenance money has gone into required and necessary improvements rather than into such niceties as beautification and comfort, much as the latter may have been desired. Had we not deferred this type of maintenance we would long since have come to the end of our financial rope.

Prior to the war, too, the North Shore sustained consistent losses. It was only through extraordinary traffic conditions that we avoided losses during the war period.

The following tabulation will show you how North Shore has fared since the war.

	Net Loss		Net Loss
1947	$ 95,792	1953	$490,971
1948	808,121	1954	488,010
1949	452,009	1955	364,253
1950	21,112	1956	344,356
1951	40,073	1957	414,914
1952	672,772	3 mos. 1958	120,179

In all, these yearly losses add up to a total of $4,312,562 in the post-war period.

3) Now in mid-1958, in the face of an impossible financial situation, we are confronted with major capital outlays far beyond our means. These are occasioned by municipal improvement programs, largely in and around Milwaukee, designed to facilitate the flow of automobile traffic. Ironically, the automobile is one of our greatest competitors and one of the prime causes of our business decline. Milwaukee is doing an excellent job of highway improvement, but one of its important projects lies directly in front of our northern terminal. It would cost us hundreds of thousands of dollars to bridge streets and readjust tracks going into the terminal. This and other track relocation, bridge extension and construction projects required to accommodate our operation to the ever-widening highways of the Chicago-to-Milwaukee area would cost more than $1,000,000—if we had the money. Which we have not.

4) The North Shore is unable to match competition. Not only are automobiles and modern highways making tremendous inroads into railroad traffic, but now a major bus company is inaugurating air conditioned bus service between Milwaukee and Chicago in direct competition to the North Shore. Our railroad competition, of course, has always had a time schedule advantage. Both the Milwaukee and the North Western lines make Milwaukee-Chicago runs from 22 to 52 minutes faster than our corresponding runs, for by the very nature of our passenger operation we must make more numerous stops and starts. At the same time, we must operate at high speeds between stops to keep up a representative schedule, and this in turn requires the maintenance of a strong, deep ballast roadbed that could support today's heaviest Diesels. This is exceedingly costly.

* * * *

These are but a few of the reasons why we have filed for abandonment of the line. Pending a final decision on our petitions, operations will be continued to the best of our ability. Unless some solution other than abandonment is developed, your recourse eventually must be to the excellent competing services.

We have done our best with limited means and under adverse circumstances. We are convinced there is no choice but the abandonment action.

* * * *

Chicago North Shore and Milwaukee Railway

Train time on the North Shore. While passengers crowded aboard a southbound train at Kenosha on a hot summer day in 1962, the conductor impatiently waited to give the motorman the highball. Moments later the big steel cars were rolling through the Wisconsin countryside at better than a mile a minute speed. WILLIAM D. MIDDLETON A "Save Your North Shore Line" poster provided a backdrop as a conductor consulted his watch during a station stop in the summer of 1959. Time was running out for Insull's interurban. FRED W. SCHNEIDER III

Late on a cold winter evening, motorman Francis Murray waited with his stool and satchel for a run to Milwaukee from the railway's Roosevelt Road terminal in Chicago. The occasion was departure of the final northbound train to Milwaukee. With the arrival of his train at Milwaukee early on the morning of January 21, 1963, more than a half century of electric interurban operation between Chicago and Milwaukee ended forever. At the top right, Fireman Apprentice Gerald Rannow achieved a dubious distinction when he became the last sailor to miss the last southbound train to Great Lakes the night the North Shore ended operations. ALL FRED L. TONNE — THE MILWAUKEE JOURNAL

The ghost of an *Electroliner* appeared in the deserted waiting room of the Milwaukee terminal the morning after the North Shore Line ended operation.—
FRED L. TONNE—THE MILWAUKEE JOURNAL

an economically viable private enterprise was a virtual impossibility. For North Shore the constantly tighter squeeze between rising wages and operating costs and comparatively static fares was aggravated by the inherent low productivity of men, equipment, and plant in what had increasingly become a commuter operation. Even at that, North Shore was paying wages substantially below those paid for comparable work by other railroads. The impact of the private automobile on the North Shore was evident in the line's long term trend of passenger traffic, which had declined from over 16 million passengers yearly in 1923 to barely four million in its last years. Despite the innovations, the imagination, and the merchandising that the railroad had put into promotion of its freight business, success had eluded the North Shore in its effort to develop a broad base of freight traffic that might have enabled the line to operate profitably.

After nearly a year of hearings, an Interstate Commerce Commission examiner, late in 1959, recommended approval of the abandonment. Protests from the Illinois Commerce Commission and commuters brought more hearings, and the ICC reversed its examiner, ordering the North Shore to keep going another year and to attempt to improve its financial position with higher fares and various economies. Increased revenues from a 23 percent fare increase were offset twice over by a simultaneous wage increase; and, to make matters worse, the opening of a new expressway into the Chicago Loop late in 1960 cost the North Shore more than 40,000 passengers a month.

Early in 1961 the North Shore, by this time losing better than half a million dollars a year, renewed its abandonment plea. More protests and more hearings followed. In May 1962, the ICC finally ground out an order that permitted the North Shore to abandon, only to postpone it indefinitely in response to still more protests. Again, in October, the Commission said North Shore could abandon. This time the end of operation was postponed while a Federal court ruled on a suit brought by commuters, the Illinois Commerce Commission, and the State of Illinois contesting ICC jurisdiction.

In November the judges ruled that the ICC did indeed have the authority to permit the abandonment, and the company set a January 21, 1963, date for the end of operation. A last ditch effort by a commuters' organization, the North Shore Commuters' Association, to raise funds to purchase and operate the railroad themselves failed.

Finally then, during the early morning hours of January 21, 1963, the big steel cars sped through the snow-clad Illinois and Wisconsin countryside for the last time as the midnight trains from Chicago and Milwaukee made the final runs. At 2:50 a.m. the last southbound train tied up at Chicago's Roosevelt Road station, and five minutes later the last North Shore train of all rolled into the Milwaukee terminal. Trolley poles were hooked down, the train crew carried the headlight and markers into the station, and lights were extinguished in the now-shabby terminal. The end had come for Sam Insull's super-interurban, and with it America's interurban era was truly over.

JOHN GRUBER

5

America's
Fastest Interurban

The unusually high standards employed in construction of the North Shore's main line northward from Waukegan to Milwaukee during 1904-1908 permitted the then-Chicago & Milwaukee Electric Railroad to assume a position of leadership in high speed operation at an early date. The company's first limited trains, which began operation between Evanston and Milwaukee early in 1909, were operated on schedules that allowed only 2 hours 15 minutes for the 73-mile journey, an average speed of better than 34 m.p.h., including all intermediate stops. Few 1909 interurbans were able to equal or excel this performance.

The massive Insull modernization program that began in 1916 greatly improved the North Shore's capability for high speed operation. New ballast and ties, heavier rail, and an extensive track resurfacing program provided a superb roadbed; and new substations and feeders furnished an ample power supply that permitted the company to fully exploit the capabilities of a fleet of splendid new steel interurbans, each powered by four motors totaling 560 horsepower and capable of top speeds in the vicinity of 80 m.p.h.

In 1919, when the North Shore began through operation over the elevated system into the Chicago Loop, initial limited schedules allowed 2 hours 35 minutes for the Chicago-Milwaukee journey. Only a year later the new *Badger Limited* was installed on a 2 hour 15 minute schedule that required an average speed of better than 38 m.p.h. for the 86-mile journey between terminals, which included the relatively slow 11-mile drag out of town over the Chicago elevated.

By 1925, when *Electric Traction* magazine began the award of its annual interurban speed trophy, the fastest North Shore limiteds were operating between Chicago and Milwaukee on 2 hour 10 minute schedules at a 39.7 m.p.h. average speed that was exceeded, by the narrowest of margins, only by the trophy-winning Galveston-Houston Electric Railway.

The serious obstacle to further improvement in North Shore schedules imposed by the severe speed restrictions on the 23-mile Shore Line Route between Evanston and Waukgan was removed in June 1926, with the opening of the new high speed cut-off through the Skokie Valley. With the exception of the limitations required in operation over the Chicago elevated system and in not quite three miles of operation through Milwaukee streets, the railway's main line between its two terminals was now almost entirely free of speed restrictions of any

During the nine years from 1925 to 1933, *Electric Traction* magazine presented its annual interurban speed trophy to the company operating America's fastest terminal-to-terminal schedule. The North Shore won the silver cup five times during the nine years and gained permanent possession in 1933. DONALD DUKE COLLECTION

On the left, the North Shore luxury train *Badger Limited* is shown passing another flyer on the newly completed Skokie Valley Route. The *Badger Limited* carried a dining car and operated northbound at breakfast time and southbound at the dinner hour. Under 1927 schedules the limited ripped off the 87 miles between Chicago and Milwaukee in 2 hours 5 minutes for an over-all average speed of 41.8 m.p.h. including intermediate stops. O. F. LEE COLLECTION Severe speed restrictions imposed by such conditions shown above on the 23-mile Shore Line Route limited the North Shore's capability for high terminal-to-terminal average speeds. Completion of the Skokie Valley Route in 1926 removed these restrictions and the way was then clear for the North Shore's emergence as America's fastest interurban. ARA MESROBIAN

The Big Speed Contest!

How does your road rank for speed?
Here's an opportunity to see yourself as others see you

The following table was compiled from actual timetables furnished by each of the roads represented, but, of course, is subject to human error. If your company is not on the list or is incorrectly represented in the table below, write in and tell us about it. This table will be printed again with corrections and additions in the November and December issues—*Editor.*

NAME OF RAILWAY	RUN	Distance	Regular Stops	Time	M. P. H. including stops	Rank by elapsed time	M. P. H. not including stops*	Rank by running time
Chicago, North Shore and Milwaukee R. R.	Chicago to Milwaukee	85.5	9	2 hrs. 9 min.	39.7	①	46.5	①
Terre Haute, Indianapolis and Eastern	Indianapolis to Crawfordsville	45.	0	1 hr. 20 min.	33.7	②	33.7	⑨
Illinois Traction System	Springfield to Mackinaw Jct.	57.2	2	1 hr. 42 min.	33.6	③	34.2	⑧
Interstate Public Service	Indianapolis to Louisville	117.02	10	3 hrs. 35 min.	32.6	④	36.0	⑥
Rochester and Syracuse R. R.	Rochester to Syracuse	87.	16	2 hrs. 43 min.	32.2	⑤	40.0	③
Waterloo, Cedar Falls and Northern Ry. Co.	Cedar Rapids to Waterloo	60.39	13	1 hr. 55 min.	31.5	⑥	40.7	②
Texas Electric	Dallas to Waco	97.19	13	3 hrs. 5 min.	31.4	⑦	36.6	⑤
Union Traction Company	Indianapolis and Muncie	56.52	6	1 hr. 50 min.	30.9	⑧	34.4	⑦
Michigan Electric Railway	Grand Rapids to Kalamazoo	49.72	2	1 hr. 33 min.	29.8	⑨	33.4	⑩
Pacific Electric	Los Angeles to Highland	64.34	16	2 hrs. 15 min.	28.5	⑩	37.5	④
Lake Shore Electric	Cleveland to Toledo	120.00	18	4 hrs. 15 min.	28.2	⑪	32.0	⑪
Detroit United Railway	Detroit to Jackson	76.24	7	3 hrs. 8 min.	24.2	⑫	26.6	⑫

*Stops have been arbitrarily figured at two minutes each.

kind; and the way was clear for the North Shore's emergence as America's fastest interurban.

The accelerated limited train schedules that accompanied the Skokie Valley Route opening gained the first place position for the North Shore in the 1927 *Electric Traction* speed cup competition, with 2 hour 5 minute Chicago-Milwaukee timings that represented a 41.8 m.p.h. terminal-to-terminal average. North Shore retained the speed title the following year, but then dropped to second place in 1929 and 1930 behind the South Shore Line, which was enjoying the benefits of an Insull-directed resurgence no less extensive than that of the North Shore itself.

Drastic schedule improvements, with its fastest trains operating between terminals at a 48 m.p.h. average, brought the silver cup back to the North Shore in 1931. North Shore retained the first place position for three consecutive years, to gain permanent possession of the award in 1933, by which time the company's fastest trains were averaging 51.27 m.p.h. between Chicago and Milwaukee.

The North Shore's dominant position in the famous *Electric Traction* speed competition, which was based upon over-all terminal-to-terminal average speeds rather than fastest intermediate timings, was all the more remarkable when North Shore operating conditions were taken into account. Not only did North Shore trains have to contend with some 14 miles of restricted speed operation over the Chicago elevated and in Milwaukee streets during their 87-mile journey, but even the fastest limited train schedules included 14 or more intermediate stops. In order to overcome these handicaps to high over-all average speeds, the North Shore operated its trains between intermediate stops on schedules that required start-to-start average speeds of as much as 70 m.p.h. Some of the fastest schedules allowed as little as 13 minutes for the 15 miles between station stops in Kenosha and Waukegan, or as little as nine minutes for the ten miles between stops in Racine and Kenosha.

In a special electric railway traction supplement to the British trade magazine, *The Railway Gazette*,

The "Big Speed Contest!" was on when *Electric Traction* magazine published the speed table shown on the left in their September 1924 issue. Texas' Galveston-Houston Electric Railway took top honors during the first two years of the contest, but thereafter the handsome silver trophy never left possession of Insull's Chicago interurbans. In the lower view a Chicago-bound *Silverliner* glides through South Upton Junction as it races along the Skokie Valley Route. BOTH DONALD DUKE COLLECTION

A North Shore motorman works air brakes and whistle cord as his heavy, powerful steel interurban train speeds over the Skokie Valley Route at better than 70 m.p.h. JOHN GRUBER The bulk of North Shore's high speed schedules were operated by the big cars. Below, refurbished in the *Silverliner* dress of recent years, a single car of late-1920 vintage dashes northward on tangent track north of Racine. WILLIAM D. MIDDLETON

With eight powerful traction motors totaling 1,000 horsepower and a free running speed of 85 m.p.h., the North Shore's two *Electroliner* trains were capable of superb high speed performance. Their delivery in 1941 enabled the line to establish the fastest Chicago-Milwaukee schedules in its history. Above, one of the streamliners accelerates on the Skokie Valley Route as it approaches Lake Bluff. DONALD DUKE COLLECTION

in 1935, the North Shore was described as "the fastest electric railway service in the world." Said the *Gazette,* "Some of the point to point bookings are probably without rival, and the timing of the hourly trains between leaving the Milwaukee suburban area and entering that of Chicago make the whole service the fastest of its kind in the world."

Throughout the depression years the North Shore continued to improve its high speed performance. In 1936, when Donald M. Steffee compiled the first of his annual speed surveys for *Railroad* magazine, the North Shore accounted for 1,572 of a total of 29,301 miles operated daily by U. S. and Canadian railroads on mile-a-minute or better schedules; and only a half dozen major U. S. trunk lines exceeded the North Shore's performance at speeds in excess of 60 m.p.h. The North Shore alone accounted for almost half of a total of 206 non-stop, over 60 m.p.h. runs listed for distances of less than

30 miles. Among the most remarkable North Shore schedules in 1936 or, for that matter, at any time in the railway's history, were those for two limited trains which allowed only 12 minutes for the 15 miles between stops in Waukegan and Kenosha, a start-to-start average speed of 75 m.p.h.! "Almost incredible," said *Railroad* magazine of these and similar performances.

Further luster was added to North Shore speed performance in 1941 when the two new *Electroliners* were placed in service on timecards that allowed as little as 1 hour 40 minutes for the journey between Milwaukee and Chicago, and the railway increased its daily total of 60 m.p.h. or better operation to almost 2,000 miles. Even during the troubled postwar years the old tradition was maintained, and at the time of its abandonment the North Shore was operating under a timecard that scheduled some 1,900 miles daily at a mile-a-minute or better.

6
Electric Fast Freight

Even at an early date in the company's history, revenues from freight and other non-passenger traffic were of considerably greater importance to the North Shore than they were to most Midwestern interurbans. As early as 1905, for example, combined freight and express revenues of nearly a quarter of a million dollars accounted for some 40 percent of the predecessor Chicago & Milwaukee Electric Railroad's total revenues.

The Chicago & Milwaukee began operating a modest express service between Evanston and Waukegan in 1902, and by 1912 the company was operating four express trains daily in each direction between Evanston and Milwaukee under contract to the United States Express Company. Much of this early express traffic consisted of milk deliveries, averaging 300 cans daily, from rural areas to Evanston and Milwaukee.

Carload freight traffic was of even greater importance to the Chicago & Milwaukee. Indeed, one of the reasons for construction of the railway's branch line from Lake Bluff to Libertyville and Rockefeller (Mundelein) during 1903-05 was to provide interchange connections for carload freight traffic with the Elgin, Joliet & Eastern and the Milwaukee Road at Rondout, and with the Wisconsin Central (Soo Line) at Rockefeller. In later years additional interchange points were established with the Chicago & North Western at Great Lakes and Niles Center, and with the Milwaukee Road at Racine. By 1910 the Chicago & Milwaukee's freight traffic

amounted to some 5,000 carloads annually, consisting largely of such bulk commodities as stone, gravel, and coal; and the company's freight equipment included two electric locomotives and more than 100 standard freight cars.

Concurrent with its massive improvement program for North Shore passenger service, the Insull management began a program for freight traffic development which produced results that were, if anything, even more dramatic.

Little more than a year after the new management took control in 1916, the North Shore inaugurated a fast merchandise despatch service for express and less-than-carload-lot freight traffic which quickly grew into a highly profitable operation. While the steam railroads took anywhere from two to eight days to handle LCL shipments between Chicago and Milwaukee, the North Shore guaranteed overnight delivery; and even though the electric line's rates were over a third higher than comparable steam road rates, the service proved to be extremely popular. Freight stations were constructed in Chicago, Milwaukee, and important intermediate cities, and the North Shore contracted with trucking companies for door-to-door pick up and delivery service.

At first, old passenger cars with their seats removed were used in the merchandise despatch service; but by 1919, when as much as 20,000 tons a month was being transported in the service, the North Shore ordered the first of a series of specially

designed merchandise despatch cars. The Cincinnati Car Company delivered 12 of the composite wood and steel cars early in 1920. Each of the 33 ton, 50 foot cars had a capacity of 20 tons. Two 140 horsepower motors, identical to those installed on the company's new passenger cars, were mounted on each of the merchandise cars, with provision for converting them to four motor cars if desired at a later date. Air braking and control equipment were also identical to that installed on North Shore passenger cars.

The North Shore, in connection with Crosby Line steamships operating between Milwaukee and Muskegon; the Grand Rapids, Grand Haven & Muskegon Railway; the Michigan Railway; and the Detroit United Railway began offering freight service between North Shore points and cities throughout southern Michigan in 1919. While steam railroad service sometimes took as long as two weeks, the interurban-steamship routing offered third-morning delivery to points as far distant as Detroit. Similar through rates and tariffs between North Shore points and Manistee and Ludington, Michigan, were offered via Pere Marquette steamship services.

Illustrated on the opposite page is express service as operated by North Shore's predecessor Chicago & Milwaukee Electric in 1902. One of the railway's first express cars, constructed by J. G. Brill, loads express at Evanston from horse-drawn wagons of the James and Johnson express companies. Until North Shore established its own merchandise despatch service for express and LCL freight in 1916, express was operated under contract to other concerns. Beginning in 1920, North Shore acquired a fleet of heavy wood and steel cars of the type shown above for this service. By 1924 the Cincinnati Car Company had delivered a total of 37 units. All were equipped for multiple unit control and were provided with motors and controls identical to those on the North Shore's standard passenger cars. Those shown above were equipped for ice refrigeration and electric heating to permit year-around perishable handling. O. F. LEE COLLECTION On the preceding two pages a North Shore articulated locomotive makes its way along the Illinois countryside. WILLIAM D. MIDDLETON.

In 1919 the North Shore began a campaign to solicit a greater share of produce traffic from farms along its line. Sidings were lengthened to accommodate an increased traffic and arrangements made to assure an adequate car supply. Representatives from the company's traffic department arranged sales meetings with farmer groups, which were held in passenger cars side-tracked at a convenient point. Within a short period after one such meeting the North Shore hauled over 100 cars of sugar beets and cabbage from a single station.

As a result of its service innovations and aggressive merchandising of freight business, North Shore revenues from freight and merchandise traffic increased even more rapidly than those from passenger traffic. By 1920 the North Shore was operating six merchandise despatch trains daily in each direction to handle the traffic, and total freight and merchandise revenues had increased by almost 700 percent over a four-year period—from barely $60,000 in 1916 to more than $470,000 in 1920.

In 1922, shortly after North Shore passenger service was extended to Chicago's South Side, the company began operating merchandise despatch service to two new South Side stations. During the same year the Cincinnati Car Company delivered another 15 wood and steel merchandise despatch cars. Generally similar to the original merchandise cars, the new equipment had provision for ice refrigeration and electric heating to permit the handling of perishable produce throughout the year. Another ten cars, equipped with four motors instead of two to permit hauling of standard freight cars, were ordered in 1923. In just the one year from 1922 to 1923, the North Shore's freight traffic increased by 40 percent, and total 1923 freight and express

revenues exceeded a million dollars for the first time in the company's history.

Because of both local ordinances and physical limitations, the North Shore's carload freight traffic was limited to points north of Highland Park until completion of the new Skokie Valley cut-off in June 1926. The new line permitted operation of standard freight equipment without restriction, and ample provision was made for team tracks and industrial development. The years following completion of the Skokie line saw a phenomenal increase in the North Shore's carload freight business. Between 1926 and 1927 the company's total freight tonnage increased by almost 30 percent to a 1927 total of 843,000 tons. Virtually all of the increase was attributed to new carload freight traffic generated on the Skokie Valley Route. Carload freight went up another 50 percent in 1928, and the following year saw a further increase of 15 percent. By 1929 total North Shore freight and express revenues had reached a record level of $1,732,000, an increase of some 29 times in just 13 years of Insull management.

In 1924 the Northern Ohio Traction & Light Company had experimentally rebuilt a standard interurban freight car with an insulated body and electrically-driven refrigeration equipment. So successful had been this pioneer mechanically-operated refrigerator car that the North Shore, in 1926, ordered five similar cars from the Cincinnati Car Company for the transportation of meats, dairy products, and other perishables in its merchandise despatch service. Each of the insulated cars was equipped with a thermostatically controlled ammonia refrigeration plant, which was powered by a 600 volt, direct current motor that took its power directly from the trolley wire. While the cars were not

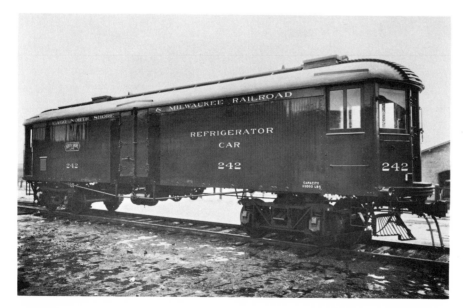

Five of these electrically-driven refrigerator cars were added to North Shore's merchandise despatch fleet in 1926. Together with a similar unit on an Ohio line, they represented the first successful use of mechanical (rather than ice) refrigeration in railroad equipment. Their use preceded by a good two decades the wide adoption of mechanically refrigerated cars on American steam railroads. O. F. LEE COLLECTION

equipped with traction motors, each of them was provided with complete control equipment and cabs at each end for operation as control trailers.

The inability of the North Shore to operate its freight cars to a downtown Chicago terminal had always constituted something of a handicap in the operation of its LCL business. When merchandise despatch service was begun in 1917, the railway had contracted with private truckers to provide pickup and delivery service at shipper expense to and from its Montrose Avenue freight station on Chicago's North Side. Later, in 1920, the railway established its own downtown Chicago freight house at Franklin and Austin streets and began trans-shipping LCL freight to the Montrose Avenue station in its own trucks. This arrangement proved costly, and in an effort to operate a more economical service the North Shore began, in 1926, the first "piggyback" trailer-on-flat-car service on any U. S. railroad.

In 1920 the North Shore established its own downtown Chicago freight house and acquired a fleet of trucks to transport LCL freight to and from the railway's Montrose Avenue freight station on Chicago's North Side. On the right is shown a view of the Chicago freight house with a line-up of new tractors and trailers. The photograph below illustrates one of North Shore's new White Motor Company Model 54 tractors and trailer. The solid rubber tires eliminated the puncture problem. BOTH WHITE MOTOR COMPANY

Although other railroads operated comparable services for horse-drawn wagons as far back as the late 19th century, North Shore's *ferry truck* service for truck trailers established in 1926 constituted the first application of modern piggyback service on any U. S. railroad. DONALD DUKE COLLECTION The equipment used was small by present-day standards, but close inspection of the 1926 photograph on the left indicates that loading and tie-down equipment differed little from modern applications. O. F. LEE COLLECTION

Special flat cars equipped with locking devices, each capable of transporting two semi-trailers, were ordered from the Standard Steel Car Company. Specially designed trailers were ordered, and those already owned by the company were modified to permit their use in the service. Loading of trailers on the flat cars was accomplished by means of ramps.

The new "ferry truck" service, as North Shore called it, proved highly successful in reducing operating costs for the railway's LCL business, and permitted the company to establish new rates which soon won a considerable volume of new business. "Ferry truck" service, for example, enabled the North Shore to gain from trucking companies traffic amounting to 500 tons monthly for a new Sears-Roebuck store in Milwaukee. Soon after the service was begun, North Shore expanded it to include pickup and delivery service in both Chicago and Milwaukee, as well as in the more important intermediate cities.

In 1932 North Shore piggyback service was again expanded to include rates for trailers owned either by common carrier truckers, or by shippers themselves, in addition to company-owned LCL trailers. Entire trucks, as well as trailers, were also carried for common carriers or private owners in the new service. The trucks were loaded two to a flat car and secured with special locking devices attached to their wheels.

The North Shore's pioneer piggyback service prospered for a number of years, reaching a peak of over 18,000 trailers handled during 1943. After the war, however, improved highways and continued growth of truck competition caused the traffic to fall off rapidly, and North Shore finally gave up the operation in 1947.

After completing work on the Rondout interchange track, where North Shore exchanged carload freight with the EJ&E *Chicago Outer Belt*, the engineer of a trio of MUed General Electric steeple cab locomotives noses his train back onto the rails of the Mundelein branch to continue westward for similar business with the Soo Line at Mundelein. BOTH WILLIAM D. MIDDLETON

Scenes of North Shore freight activity. On the right, a switchman guides a cut of cars into the EJ&E interchange track at Rondout. JOHN GRUBER Below, a rush hour Mundelein train heads west as a trio of steeple cab locomotives work the Rondout interchange. WILLIAM D. MIDDLETON Heading a consist off the Mundelein branch, the same steeple cab trio accelerates through Lake Bluff in the illustration at the upper left. DONALD DUKE COLLECTION One of the two unusual trolley-battery locomotives added to the North Shore's motive power roster is shown in the lower left. The first of their kind ever built, they were capable of operation from either the overhead trolley wire or batteries, which permitted the railway to serve industrial sidings without requiring the costly installation of overhead wire. A single battery charge provided enough juice to haul a 33-car train a distance of five miles at 12 m.p.h. DONALD DUKE COLLECTION

North Shore's freight power was augmented in 1947 with the purchase of two 100 ton, 16-wheeled locomotives from the Oregon Electric Railway. Each of the 59-foot locomotives was powered by eight traction motors with a combined output of 1120 horsepower. One of them, box cab No. 458, is shown at speed with a southbound main line freight at Racine. ARA MESRO-BIAN The impressive dimensions and unusual articulated arrangement of the locomotive are evident in the broadside study on the right. WILLIAM D. MIDDLETON

Even though the North Shore had entered into carload freight interchange with steam railroads at an early date, it by no means escaped the hostility so often displayed towards the interurbans by steam railroads. Perhaps the earliest manifestation of this was in the "cabbage" case of 1907. The then-Chicago & Milwaukee had succeeded in establishing joint rates for cabbages and other freight from points on its line to points on the Illinois Central and its connections. Upon protest of the competing Chicago & North Western, the Illinois Central cancelled the new rates. The Chicago & Milwaukee appealed the cancellation to the Interstate Commerce Commission, which ruled in favor of the steam lines, basing its decision upon the contention that the territory was already adequately served by the older carriers.

In 1940 the North Shore went before the ICC with a case in which far more serious issues were involved. Indeed, had the Commission ruled in favor of the steam railroads, early abandonment of the interurban was a not unlikely consequence. The case, which involved four other Midwestern interurbans and a Minnesota short line, the Minneapolis, Northfield & Southern Railway, as well as the North Shore, resulted from a 1938 decision by the Western Trunk Line Committee, a steam road group, to cancel through rates and tariffs which involved the North Shore and the other short lines as intermediate or "bridge" carriers.

By the late 1930's carload freight had assumed a greatly increased importance to the North Shore. The decline in freight revenues during the depression years had been nowhere near as great as the corresponding decline in passenger revenues; and by 1937, when North Shore gross operating revenues were barely half of the 1929 level, freight revenues of well over a million dollars accounted for nearly 28 percent of the total. A large part of this freight business was represented by carload traffic in which the North Shore was an overhead or "bridge" carrier, receiving shipments from one steam road connection and delivering them to another. In the case of its connections with the North

The second of North Shore's two former Oregon Electric articulated locomotives — No. 459 — was virtually identical except for a steeple cab arrangement. Because of better visibility from the center cab during switching operations, No. 459 was usually preferred over its box cab sister. On the left, No. 459 heads a westbound manifest for the Rondout interchange. DONALD DUKE COLLECTION Below, the "alligator" as some called it, working the Milwaukee Road interchange track at Racine. WILLIAM D. MIDDLETON On the right, No. 459 is seen wheeling tonnage south of Zion on the main line. The double trolley poles were required to draw sufficient current for the eight traction motors. DONALD DUKE COLLECTION

Western and the Milwaukee Road, the interurban sometimes delivered traffic at one interchange point to the same carrier from which it had received it at another.

Good service and vigorous promotion had developed this overhead traffic to a record level by 1937, when the 24,426 cars of intermediate freight handled by the North Shore produced almost a third of the railway's freight revenue and nearly 8 percent of its total operating revenues. Had the steam railroads been successful in their effort to recapture this traffic, the effect on the North Shore, which had been losing money steadily since 1931, would have been disastrous. Fortunately, the ICC ruled in favor of the electric line and prevented the steam roads from carrying out the cancellation, with the exception of through routings under which the North Shore returned carload traffic to the same carrier from which it had been received, which the Commission ruled could be discontinued.

Despite the phenomenal growth of North Shore freight traffic under the Insull management, the rail-way ultimately failed to develop a broad base of freight business, comparable, for example, to that of the Insull-managed Chicago South Shore & South Bend Railroad, which would have permitted the company to become an integral part of the national railway network and which would have generated sufficient profit to offset the losses incurred in an increasingly uneconomic passenger operation. Much of the spectacular growth in freight business during the Insull era was represented by short haul LCL traffic transported in the North Shore's merchandise despatch service, which proved particularly vulnerable to truck competition in later years and was given up altogether in 1947. The boom in carload business from on-line industries which followed completion of the Skokie Valley Route ended with the onset of the depression, and the company was never able to secure more than about 100 on-line industries. Even the promising "bridge" traffic in carload freight proved to have limits, and from the beginning of the depression onward the company's annual freight revenues seldom exceeded much more than a million dollars, and no amount of traffic promotion seemed able to make any significant improvement.

7

Disaster at Highway 43

JOHN GRUBER

Despite its high operating speeds and unusual density of traffic, the North Shore was remarkably free of the serious accidents that were all too often a proclivity of interurban railways. Even during its early years, before the general installation of automatic block signals and other safety devices, the North Shore enjoyed a remarkable safety record.

In 1911, for example, E. E. Downs, general manager of the then Chicago & Milwaukee Electric Railroad, was able to call attention to the fact that during the company's first 13 years of operation, during which time it had transported between 75,000,000 and 100,000,000 passengers, not a single fatality had resulted from its operations. Remarked Mr. Downs with pardonable pride, "I do not think there is another railroad in America, either steam or electric, which has been in operation the same length of time or carried the same number of people that can show a record as clean."

The vigorous safety program begun by the Insull management in 1917 enhanced even this achievement, and within only a few years the North Shore enjoyed one of the finest safety records in the entire industry. Unfortunately, the North Shore was handicapped by an excessive number of highway grade crossings; by 1921 there were some 150 of them on the entire system. As the ownership and operation of private automobiles became increasingly general, it was almost inevitable then, despite the most vigilant safety program and the substantial investment of the Insull management in protective gates and signals, that grade crossing collisions between motor vehicles and high speed trains should become an altogether-too-frequent occurrence. Indeed, one such collision, on February 23, 1930, resulted in the most serious and tragic accident in North Shore history.

The morbid poster above produced during a North Shore safety campaign of the early 1920's, typified an event which occurred with unhappy frequency on the grade crossing-burdened interurban despite a substantial investment in protective devices and safety education. ARTHUR D. DUBIN COLLECTION One of North Shore's progressive research projects was a barrier type crossing protector with "telltale"-like warning signals. The "telltale" swung across the road prior to the trains arrival as shown in the top left view. Should the motorist pass through the "telltale" warning, another barrier was lowered from between the two big steel arches. This trapped the motor vehicle before the speeding interurban train reached the crossing. BOTH DONALD DUKE COLLECTION

Twisted rails and jacknifed interurban cars littered the right-of-way near Kenosha in the aftermath of the most spectacular wreck in North Shore history. Had it not been for the massive construction of the heavy steel cars involved, loss of life might have been far greater. Rails and right-of-way were torn up and overhead ripped down for a distance of several hundred feet. ALL O. F. LEE COLLECTION The grisly tangle on the right occurred on the Chicago "L" in 1936, when a towerman's error sent a fast-moving North Shore steel train into an almost stationary wooden elevated car. CHICAGO TRIBUNE—O. F. LEE COLLECTION

The accident occurred at the Highway 43 crossing near the northwest limits of Kenosha, Wisconsin, late one Sunday evening. A Milwaukee motorist, traveling at an estimated speed of 50 to 60 m.p.h., disregarded warning signals and swerved around another automobile already stopped at the crossing in an attempt to beat a northbound, 16-car merchandise despatch freight train to the crossing. The driver was apparently unaware of a Milwaukee-Chicago limited train approaching from the north at a speed of 70 m.p.h., which struck the automobile and hurled the crushed wreckage of the Buick sedan 200 feet down the right-of-way. Initially, the five cars of the passenger train remained on the rails. The force of the impact, however, caused them to sway from side to side and the third car sideswiped a car of the northbound freight, causing the entire passenger train, and most of the freight train, to derail. The five derailed passenger cars tore up the track for a distance of over a block, ripped down overhead wires, and finally jackknifed at the bottom of an eight foot embankment. The sound of the impact was heard over a half a mile away, and the arcing of downed high tension wires could be seen in downtown Kenosha, several miles away.

Both the motorist and a passenger in his car were killed. Ten others were killed, and 95 injured, among the crews of the two trains and the 150 passengers on the Chicago limited. All five of the 700 class interurban cars involved were badly damaged, one of them so severely that it was never rebuilt. Although a coroner's jury found the North Shore entirely blameless in the disaster, the company voluntarily decided to make settlements with the victims.

Another source of several severe North Shore accidents was the railway's operation over the Chicago elevated system, which even into recent years has been notably deficient in modern safety devices. The worst "L" crash in which the North Shore figured occurred on a foggy Thanksgiving eve on November 24, 1936, when a towerman's error sent an elevated train onto a wrong track. The crowded "L" train, just leaving a station, was overtaken by a North Shore train moving at about 40 m.p.h. The North Shore train was made up of steel equipment, as was most of the "L" train, but unfortunately the rear car of the elevated train was of wooden construction, and was almost completely telescoped by the lead car of the North Shore train. Eleven persons, all of them passengers in the demolished wooden car, were killed and some 35 were injured. It was the worst elevated crash in Chicago history.

Twenty years later, on November 5, 1956, the North Shore figured in another, remarkably similar, "L" wreck, when a North Shore train, stopped at the Wilson Avenue station, was rammed from behind by an elevated train. Eight "L" passengers were killed and some 200 persons were injured.

8   Electroliner

In constructing the two streamlined *Electroliners,* which were introduced in the North Shore's Chicago-Milwaukee service in February 1941, builder St. Louis Car Company had faced an almost impossible set of specifications. The North Shore wanted a high speed luxury streamliner that could hold its own against the new *Hiawatha* and *400* competition of its steam road rivals. Yet the trains had to trundle, trolley car fashion, through Milwaukee streets, and had to contend with the severe restrictions of the Chicago elevated system, where minimum radius curves of 90 feet were encountered and high level platforms limited car width to only 8 feet 8 inches.

St. Louis Car produced an ingenious solution to the design problem. The curvature restrictions were solved by designing a four section articulated train 155 feet 4 inches in length, and the width limitation was overcome by the adoption of a "fish belly" cross section which bulged out above the platform level to a maximum width of 9 feet 2 inches. Welded high-tensile steel construction held the total weight of each train to only 210,500 pounds, no more than that of two of the North Shore's standard steel cars.

Roller bearing-equipped cast steel trucks were employed, and eight motors totaling 1,000 horsepower provided sufficient power for a free running speed of 85 m.p.h. With the use of field shunting, the trains were capable of speeds in excess of 100 m.p.h. Electric braking, supplemented by air brakes, was installed, and the "all electric" trains were equipped with electro-pneumatic controls.

Extensive use was made of rubber cushioning, car bodies were provided with three inches of insulation, and floors were covered with heavy, felt-cushioned rubber tile to provide an unusually low sound level. The fully air conditioned trains were provided with high capacity ventilating systems and electric heating.

Each *Electroliner* was provided with luxury coach accommodations seating a total of 120 passengers. Interiors of the trains were decorated in color schemes of coral, blue, and silver; scarlet and gray; or apricot and turquoise. One unit of each train was given over to a tavern-lounge section seating 26, where beverage and light meal service was provided. Heavy carpeting was laid on the floor of the tavern-lounge, which was finished in soft brown, coral, and gold. Fanciful red and green birds, giraffes, elephants, and other animals decorated the walls. Waiters were outfitted in special uniforms of British tan and brown.

As evidenced by these builder's interior photographs, the North Shore's incomparable *Electroliner* trains afforded 1941 interurban travelers accommodations that rivaled contemporary steam railroad streamliners. Above, the tavern-lounge section, and below, the women's coach and the regular coach in the lower view. TOP AND BOTTOM—ST. LOUIS CAR DIVISION OF GENERAL STEEL INDUSTRIED. CENTER COURTESY RAILROAD MAGAZINE

Fresh from the paint shop of the St. Louis Car Company, an *Electroliner* train was posed for one of the first record photographs. ST. LOUIS CAR DIVISION OF GENERAL STEEL INDUSTRIES Between Milwaukee and Waukegan the North Shore's vest pocket electric streamliner travelled a typical interurban right-of-way. At the right, with controller wide open and air horn blasting, a southbound "super-interurban" ripped across Four Mile Road north of Racine. RICHARD J. SOLOMON

Delivered from the builder early in 1941, the *Electroliners* were introduced with a publicity fanfare that recalled some of the more extravagant affairs of the Insull era. An electric "Welcome Electroliners" sign was mounted on the tower of the Milwaukee city hall, banners were placed on the marquees of leading Milwaukee hotels, and 400 Milwaukee streetcars carried head end signs welcoming the new trains. Huge crowds toured the *Electroliners* during public exhibitions at Milwaukee, Racine, Kenosha, Waukegan, and Chicago.

On February 6, 1941, the two trains, one operating from Milwaukee and the other from Chicago, made a special trip over the line carrying 27 mayors or community heads from every community along the North Shore, numerous other dignitaries, and nearly 50 radio and newspaper men. Departure of the southbound special from Milwaukee was celebrated with a ceremonial ribbon cutting by Mayor Ziedler, who was attended by 28 aldermen and city officials.

Shortly before noon the two trains met at Glen Flora siding in Waukegan, and the party adjourned to the nearby Glen Flora Country Club for a round of congratulatory speeches and an elaborate filet mignon luncheon hosted by the railway.

Entering regular service later in the month on the fastest Chicago-Milwaukee schedules in North Shore history, the *Electroliners* proved to be an unqualified success. St. Louis Car had produced equipment which equalled or exceeded every expectation, and the *Electroliners* represented, without question, the finest interurban passenger equipment ever constructed in North America. Regular as clockwork the two trains ripped off five daily round trips between the two cities with hardly an interruption for more than two decades; and in their lifetime on the North Shore, which ended only with the abandonment of the railway, each of the *Electroliners* accumulated a remarkable total of nearly three and a half million revenue miles.

Above, an *Electroliner* passenger enjoys a light breakfast as the streamliner races through open countryside. At the right, a motorman and conductor compare watches during a brief stop at Kenosha. BOTH WILLIAM D. MIDDLETON On the opposite page an *Electroliner* thunders across the massive steel structure spanning the Root River north of Racine. RICHARD J. SOLOMON

A pictorial panorama of *Electroliners* in action. At left, an inbound *Electroliner* slips past "L" platforms at the Lake and Wells junction on the famous Chicago Loop. Towering office buildings overshadowed the busy elevated steel highway. RICHARD J. SOLOMON Below, northbound from Chicago at a speed well in excess of a mile a minute, a North Shore streamliner races through verdant Illinois countryside near Zion. FRED W. SCHNEIDER III On the lower right, the motorman and conductor of an *Electroliner* wait at Racine for passengers to board at the rear entrance before resuming their journey to Milwaukee. WILLIAM D. MIDDLETON Underway at high speed, the electric streamliner briefly shatters the calm of a hot summer afternoon as it flashes past a lonely Wisconsin farmhouse. DONALD DUKE COLLECTION

JOHN GRUBER

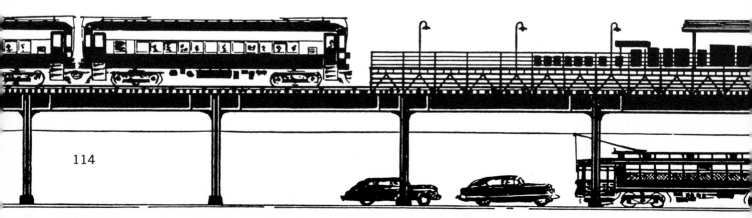

9

The "L" and the Loop

GEORGE CLOFF — COURTESY OF TRAINS MAGAZINE

The North Shore's Chicago entry over the elevated railway system, which permitted convenient North Side and Loop stops, gave the railway a decided competitive advantage over its steam road competitors. Although the famous elevated Loop, which gave the downtown section of Chicago its name was completed in 1897, North Shore trains did not enjoy the use of the facility until 1919. Shortly afterward, the new Uptown station at Wilson and Broadway, shown in the view on the left, was built jointly by the North Shore and the Chicago Rapid Transit. A large lobby at street level housed ticket offices, while attractive shops were grouped around the sides. DONALD DUKE COLLECTION Reflections of a late afternoon sun on well-polished rails create a pattern of concentric circles as a North Shore train swings around a tight "L" curve on the North Side in the center view. With a deceiving air of nonchalance a North Shore trainman raises the trolley pole and somehow manages to land the shoe on the overhead wire as a train speeds past the end of third rail territory at Crawford Avenue on the Skokie Valley Route. BOTH JOHN GRUBER Below, a North Shore *Silverliner* bound for Chicago rolls into Howard Street station where North Shore's "L" trackage rights began. DONALD DUKE COLLECTION

Two young passengers enjoy the second-story view from a North Shore interurban rumbling into Chicago over the elevated. JOHN GRUBER On the right, a Mundelein-bound train just out of the North Shore's Roosevelt Road terminal curves northward toward the Loop on the Wabash Street "L" structure. WILLIAM D. MIDDLETON

The Lake Michigan shoreline traveled by North Shore trains has long been noted for uncommonly severe winter weather, and winter was always a trying time for the railway. Even during the North Shore's last days of operation the trains battled bitter cold and unusually severe snow storms. Blowing snow obscured the Chicago skyline as a two-car southbound train rolled through the Loyola Avenue "L" station during a January 1963 blizzard. GREG HEIER

118

Top, above, a Milwaukee-bound train pulls into the Howard Street station alongside a big electrical side exhorting motorists in the street below to "travel North Shore". The view above illustrates a typical North Side stop on the elevated route followed by North Shore trains. Above, right, a Milwaukee train squeals around a tight curve while a city-bound train of lightweight "L" cars rolls by. On the right, the massive Merchandise Mart towers over a train of *Silverliner* equipment traveling northward over the elevated. ALL DONALD DUKE

10 Highwood

The Chicago & Milwaukee Electric established its shops, carbarn, power plant, and general offices at Highwood, Illinois, in 1898. Highwood remained the railway's operating center until its abandonment in 1963. The handsome Colonial style headquarters building shown on the left was completed in 1905. In addition to company offices the building contained reading, smoking and locker rooms for trainmen, and a basement gymnasium. DONALD DUKE COLLECTION The view above illustrates the Highwood storage yard which paralleled the Shore Line Route main line and the passenger line of the Chicago & North Western. The general offices are in the background. GEORGE KRAMBLES COLLECTION On the right, this spinning motor-generator at the Highwood power plant fed 600 volt direct current power to the trolley wire around 1912. PAUL STRINGHAM COLLECTION In the lower view, a steel interurban passes through the new automatic car washer installed at Highwood in 1930. CHARLES GOETHE COLLECTION

For more than 60 years Highwood's skilled shop forces repaired, rebuilt, and modernized the big interurban cars. Above and at right are representative views of shop activity. TOP, LEFT AND RIGHT WILLIAM D. MIDDLETON—RIGHT DAVID A. STRASSMAN, COURTESY OF TRAINS MAGAZINE The last major modernization program carried out at Highwood was the conversion of some 30 steel cars of the Insull era into *Silverliner* units during the 1950's. Two of the first red and silver cars completed under the program are shown at left in 1950. CHARLES GOETHE COLLECTION In the lower view a general panorama of the Highwood shops taken in 1923. While increasing numbers of steel cars were coming into use, wooden equipment was still plentiful. O. F. LEE COLLECTION

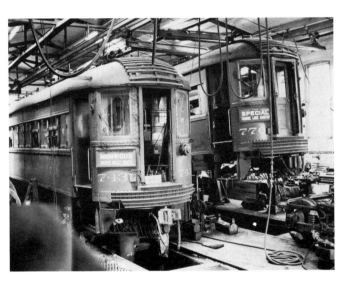

11 Rolling Stock

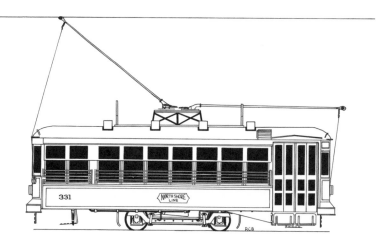

BIRNEYS 326 - 337

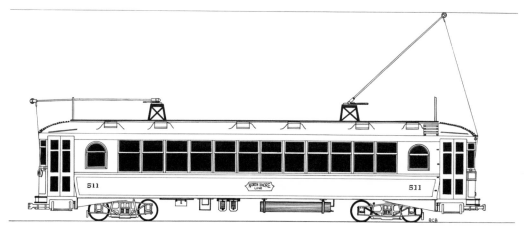

LIGHTWEIGHT COACHES 510 and 511

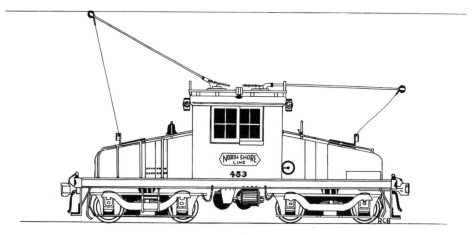

LOCOMOTIVES 452 - 454

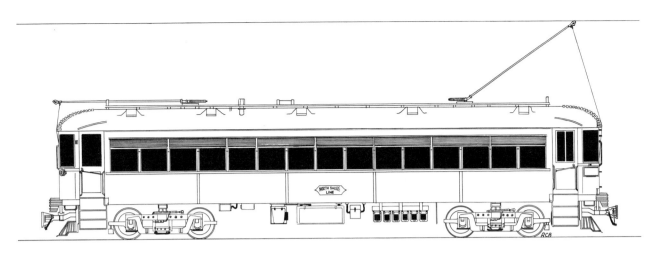

INTERURBAN COACHES 150 - 164

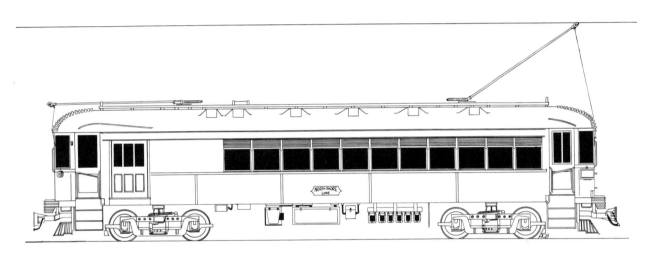

COMBINATION COACHES 250 - 256

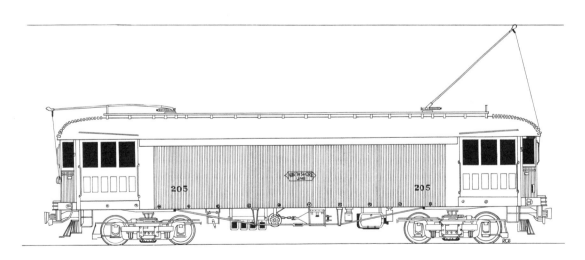

EXPRESS & MERCHANDISE 203 - 214

Electroliner Reprise

When North Shore ended operations in January 1963 it seemed that all was over for the railway's incomparable *Electroliners,* and the two trains joined a forlorn lineup of North Shore rolling stock that awaited the scrapper's torch or, at best, honorable retirement at some trolley museum. Then, in September 1963 came the happy news that Philadelphia Suburban Transportation Company had purchased the trains for operation over its high-speed, third rail Norristown Division, the former Philadelphia & Western Railroad. Soon afterward the *Electroliners* rolled eastward over C&NW and PRR rails to join the Red Arrow Lines' celebrated Brill "Bullet" fleet.

PSTCo's Upper Darby shops stripped off old paint, ironed out the dents accumulated in long service, and repainted the streamliners in a new deep red and white color scheme. Floors were renewed and seats reupholstered in charcoal, sapphire, gold, black, and rust fabrics. Side walls were refinished in peach, chocolate, gray, and turquoise, and ceiling were done in bone white. Trolley poles were removed, third rail shoes adapted for the PSTCo third rail system, and the door arrangement modified to accommodate Red Arrow's lower, limited length platforms.

A network of speakers for tape recorded music was installed in each train, and Red Arrow took out a liquor license and laid plans to provide commuters with breakfast in the morning and hard liquor in the afternoon from the tavern-lounge section. The Red Arrow refurbishing even extended to new names, and the two trains were re-christened the *Liberty Liners* "Valley Forge" and "Independence Hall".

Finally, all was in readiness, and on January 31, 1964, the refurbished *Liberty Liners* entered regular 69th Sreet-Norristown service over the 13.5-mile Norristown Division. Suburban Philadelphia had a new standard of commuter service and electric traction's finest trains were off and running again. There was even heady talk from PSTCo president Merritt H. Taylor, Jr. of extending *Liberty Liner* service another 21 miles westward to King of Prussia and Downington via trackage rights over the Reading Company's Chester Valley branch.

Inbound from Norristown, the "Valley Forge" approached the Villanova Junction interlocking tower as shown on the left. The tower once guarded the junction with the Strafford Branch, abandoned in 1956. In the above view, waiting passengers on the inbound platform gawk as the "Valley Forge" accelerates away from a Bryn Mawr station stop on the way to Norristown. ALL PHOTOGRAPHS BY AARON G. FRYER.

Northbound to Norristown, the "Independence Hall" in the upper left flashes through Rosemont two days after the beginning of regular *Liberty Liner* service. In the upper right, Norristown-bound from 69th Street Terminal, the "Valley Forge" leans into superelevated curvature at Radnor. Below, the southbound "Independence Hall" glides past comfortable suburban dwellings approaching a station stop at Bryn Mawr two days after regular *Liberty Liner* operation began.

JOHN GRUBER

LAYOUT - DON DUKE

HALFTONES - AL ROSE